NEW JERSEY
STATE OF MIND

NEW JERSEY
STATE OF MIND

PETER GENOVESE

Rutgers University Press

New Brunswick, Camden, and Newark, New Jersey, and London

Library of Congress Cataloging-in-Publication Data

Names: Genovese, Peter, 1952- author.
Title: New Jersey state of mind / Peter Genovese.
Description: New Brunswick : Rutgers University Press, 2020. | Includes index.
Identifiers: LCCN 2019034604 | ISBN 9781978803909 (hardcover) | ISBN
9781978803916 (epub) | 9781978803930 (web pdf) | ISBN 9781978803923
(mobi)
Subjects: LCSH: New Jersey—Description and travel.
Classification: LCC F134.6 .G465 2020 | DDC 917.49—dc23
LC record available at https://lccn.loc.gov/2019034604

A British Cataloging-in-Publication record for this book is available from the
British Library.

All photographs by the author

♾ The paper used in this publication meets the requirements of the
American National Standard for Information Sciences—Permanence of Paper
for Printed Library Materials, ANSI Z39.48-1992.

www.rutgersuniversitypress.org

Manufactured in the United States of America

CONTENTS

NEW JERSEY
STATE OF MIND

INTRODUCTION

I LIVE, BREATHE, EVEN DREAM New Jersey. In the past 35 years, I have driven a million and a half miles around the state for stories, first for the *Home News* (later the *Home News Tribune*) in Central Jersey and, for the past 20 years, for the *Star-Ledger* and nj.com.

I've written thousands of stories and seven books about the Garden State. The latter include *Jersey Diners*, *Roadside New Jersey*, and *The Jersey Shore Uncovered: A Revealing Season on the Beach* for Rutgers University Press and *Food Lovers' Guide to New Jersey* for Globe Pequot Press. At some point, I have written something about all 565 municipalities in the state, plus countless towns and villages.

I know New Jersey.

Not New Jersey politics or sports or community news but New Jersey as a place. Every nook and cranny and corner. And I know how to get there without a GPS, which you will never find in my Jeep.

Which brings us to this book. It's inspired by a series that appeared in the *Star-Ledger* beginning in October 2010 called Jersey State of Mind. This is what I wrote in the introductory piece:

> The stories will take you all over Jersey, celebrating the state in all its variety and diversity, illuminating corners you never visited, or knew existed. The real Jersey, not the cliched, stereotypical or rose-tinted one.

The resulting stories had a strong sense of place, with detail that put you on the scene. Most of the stories were written by the reporters in the paper's features department, of which I was a part. When it came time to pitch this book to Rutgers University Press, I talked about that sense of place, that celebration of the state in all its variety and diversity. Props to Peter Mickulas, executive editor at Rutgers University Press, for being excited about this project right from the beginning.

For this book, I spent months combing the state for good stories, those that would reveal New Jersey's uniqueness, diversity, and specialness. Profiles of interesting people and places, stories that would speak to the character and sometimes gritty charm of this state. This is not the Chamber of Commerce's or the state Division of Travel and Tourism's version of

New Jersey, just real everyday Jersey. None of the stories have previously appeared in the *Star-Ledger* or on nj.com.

Do these chapters tell the entire story of New Jersey? No, of course not. But I think they reveal more of this state as it is today than any other book—and certainly more than my other books. There are no politicians or high-profile or "important" people in this book, just everyday folks who contribute to the diverse fabric that is New Jersey.

You'll meet a female craft brewer, the captain of the state's official tall ship, demolition derby drivers, a Food Network personality, the owners of a legendary Italian ice stand, the disc jockeys at the nation's largest South Asian radio station, the owner of an old-fashioned amusement park, the makers of a strange and wonderful elixir called Boost!, and the folks who monitor traffic on the Garden State Parkway and New Jersey Turnpike.

Among many others.

If this book is fun and vibrant and colorful, it's because of them. Thanks to all of them for letting me tell their stories. No state has been more mocked, misunderstood, and maligned than New Jersey, as I've long maintained. This is one attempt to correct those misconceptions. If you're from here, I hope this book will introduce you to a New Jersey you're not familiar with.

If you're from elsewhere, here is my message: this is what we're about.

THE SWAMPS OF NORTH JERSEY

MIDMORNING, HACKENSACK RIVER, AND NO-SEE-UMS are picnicking on my right arm. I'm thinking, Didn't the instructions emailed earlier in the week say I shouldn't worry about bugs? I'm in the fabled swamps of North Jersey, about to take a cruise of sorts through New Jersey's most unlikely urban wilderness. The Meadowlands—32 square miles and 8,500 acres of water, marsh, and open space four miles from Manhattan.

Ever hike or boat through it? Didn't think so.

I'm at River Barge Park & Marina in Carlstadt, on the other side of the New Jersey Turnpike from MetLife Stadium, about to take one of the "eco-cruises" run by Hackensack Riverkeeper. Most of the organization's river cruises launch from Laurel Hill Park in Secaucus. Today, we depart from River Barge Park, reached by a bumpy dirt road that includes a dilapidated-looking but still-functioning boat club that doesn't appear on Google Maps. "We'll be heading upriver first," Bill Sheehan tells the passengers on one of Hackensack Riverkeeper's pontoon boats. "Lots of stuff going on. Keep your binoculars ready, your bazookas"—he looks at a birder with a camera lens nearly as long as a baseball bat—"or whatever you call them."

Ah, the rock 'n' roll vampire speaks.

That's how he describes his teens and early 20s, when he played the drums in a series of bands, including Gretchen, Crayon, and Casper. Never heard of them? Me neither.

"You'd get up at three in the afternoon and not get to sleep until six the next morning," he recalls. "I was out six, seven nights a week, rocking and rolling. I was not getting rich; I was not getting dead." He left the music business with his soul "intact" when disco appeared; he refused to play the "monotonous drone" disco required.

"Bill, Bill, Bill!" shouts Bazooka Guy. "The peregrine [falcon] is under the bridge."

"Indeed it is," Sheehan replies. He sports an earring in his left ear and a big bushy mustache and wears a tiki shirt resplendent with parrots and toucans, shark-dotted white shorts, and a cap that says "Make America Green Again." A Peterson Field Guide is stuffed into a corner of the boat dashboard. He was born to be on the water—his father, Frank, was a barge captain; his grandfather, a dock foreman. But not right away. He spent 10 years as a cab driver. One day, he was watching a fishing show on ESPN; there was a short segment on the San Francisco Baykeeper.

"I saw the image of this guy in a rowboat, paddling between these huge tankers, writing down registration numbers," Sheehan recalls. "I thought, 'How can I get a job like that?' I was intrigued by someone representing an entire ecosystem."

He worked as a volunteer for the New York / New Jersey Baykeeper program and then in 1997 founded Hackensack Riverkeeper. In 1998, he acquired a pontoon boat, then two canoes, and convinced the then-county executive that Laurel Hill Park in Secaucus would be a great place for a canoe operation.

"There's an egret flying across the river," he says, scanning the skies. "Also, osprey with a fish in its mouth."

The Hackensack River is an unlikely oasis of beauty, minutes from the New Jersey Turnpike and New York City.

About 65 species of breeding bird, including the northern harrier and osprey, can be found here. Another 200 species, including bald eagles, use the Meadowlands as a migratory stopover.

"It's a very important stop on the North American flyway," Sheehan says. Hackensack Riverkeeper is about much more than just taking birders with huge camera lenses out on boat rides, though. The program's main mission is to protect, preserve, and restore the river and its watershed. It's an area with a horrible history.

In the 1960s and 1970s, the Meadowlands was a national eyesore, a dumping ground for garbage, chemicals, and more than a few dead bodies. James Hoffa may or may not be buried out there somewhere. "A swampy, mosquito-infested jungle where rusting auto bodies, demolition rubble, industrial oil slicks and cattails merge in unholy, stinking union," read a 1978 federal report. Berry's Creek, which we will pass later, was called the nation's most polluted waterway in the late 1970s.

The pontoon boat turns into Sawmill Creek. How bad was pollution back then?

"There was raw sewage in the river all the time," he replies. "Industrial waste was dumped into the water all the time." He acknowledges he can be a "horrible" adversary but adds that he can also be "very open-minded and pragmatic. There are people out there who think nothing should ever be built again in the Meadowlands." He's not one of them; he was a supporter of Xanadu, the failed retail and entertainment complex now being resurrected as American Dream.

The riverkeeper conducts 25–30 cleanups per season. "Some of our volunteers are religious about it," Sheehan says. "They don't want the season to end." He and Hugh Carola, the Riverkeeper program director, conduct about 50 eco-cruises from May through October. There are three routes: the lower tidal reaches of the Hackensack River, the southern Meadowlands to the city of Hackensack, and down the river to the entire length of Newark Bay.

All passengers are emailed instructions beforehand. Bring a jacket; temperatures are usually 5–10 degrees cooler on the water. Alcohol is OK "in moderation." Cruises are not conducted in the rain. Bring insect repellant, not for mosquitos but for the "annoying" gnats. Ah, I may have misread that part. My favorite paragraph: "Leave the Dramamine home. Our 30-foot pontoon boats are very stable and we travel on relatively calm waters. We've never had a case of seasickness."

Our boat chugs past the sports complex, then the Bergen County utilities plant. "See the egrets sitting up there?" Sheehan says. "They love this area."

The river's biggest current threat? A 1200-megawatt gas-powered plant planned for North Bergen "for the exclusive use of New York," Sheehan points out. "New Jersey gets all the pollution. It sounds like a good deal, right? It's another attempt by the fossil fuel industry to keep us hooked on gas and oil to the end of the 21st century."

"Another Meadowlands Scam" was the headline on the lead story in the summer 2018 issue of *Hackensack Tidelines*, published quarterly by Hackensack Riverkeeper. It detailed a community information meeting to oppose that gas-fired power plant in North Bergen.

The plant "will be polluting NJ's already compromised air in order to send electricity to New York City alone," according to the story. "It could generate nearly 2.4 million metric tons of carbon dioxide a year in an area that already fails to meet national Clean Water Act quality standards . . . the project would put our waterways at risk. It would add over eight million gallons of wastewater a day to the already taxed sewer system."

"No state in this country would need a riverkeeper if the government was doing its job," Sheehan says. "This is about holding everyone's feet to the fire, from the local public officials to the developers to the citizens who, over the years, allowed this to happen."

When the boat tours started, he says, "people looked at me like I was crazy."

About 80,000 people have taken the tours over the years. "Number of egrets hanging here, working the edge [of the riverbank]," he announces. "Look at this—flock of cormorants flying at us. No, they're geese. Dopey geese, get going." Besides birds, there are raccoons, skunks, squirrels, possums, red fox, coyote, diamond terrapins, and snapping turtles lurking out here. Bet you didn't know that New Jersey boasts the highest density of wildlife per square mile of any state.

We pass under a counterbalanced bridge with a mammoth concrete weight that looks poised to drop on the next NJ Transit train. The boat bogs down then sputters to a halt.

"We're overweight," he tells the captain of another boat. "Can you take a couple people?"

"We have oars," the captain jokes. Several passengers on our boat volunteer to board the other boat, and soon we're off again. At one point, Sheehan points out an osprey nest on a bridge, one of 14 osprey nests on the river.

One thing you won't find out here—mosquitos, at least not in force. It's toward the end of the cruise season, and Sheehan's can of Off! is still close to full.

The swamps of North Jersey are beautiful, quiet, soothing, and a bit spooky. You can see the turnpike traffic but not hear it. Fish inhabiting the river include striped bass and bluefish.

"The biggest problem in this river right now is sediment at the bottom of the river . . . polluted by PCBs and dioxin," according to Sheehan. "We advise people not to eat the fish. You could catch striped bass and take it home and cook it and it would taste wonderful, but you have to worry about the long-term effects of dioxin and PCBs.

"My work is not finished until this water is sustainable and fishable, and by fishable, I mean you can take that fish home and cook it," he adds. Sheehan says he'll stay on the job as long as his health "doesn't go south." The job, he says, "has made me young again. It has literally energized me. The saddest day of my life will be the day I can't do it anymore."

KING OF THE ROLLING CHAIRS

JACK TAIMANGLO WAVES A COPY of an *Atlantic City Press* full-page ad for a book on the world's most famous boardwalk. One of the six photos in the ad is of rolling chairs on the boardwalk on a perfect summer day. He finds this ironic because the paper has called for the chairs' end, arguing that "they are doing the city's image more harm than good . . . the chairs have to go."

"I get too emotional when I get to talking about this," Taimanglo says. Ted Garry, standing next to Taimanglo in a parking lot across the street from Stiletto, a gentleman's club, smiles. He's known Taimanglo many years; they keep their rolling chairs in a storage space under the boardwalk, steps from where we're standing.

"Saltwater taffy and rolling chairs—it's something people expect to see when they go up to the boardwalk," Garry will say later. "It's a tradition I want to preserve."

The rolling chairs, though, may be on borrowed time. They first appeared on the Atlantic City Boardwalk in 1884. M. D. Shill, a Philadelphia manufacturer of perambulators, opened a store in Atlantic City to rent out baby carriages and invalid chairs "for convalescents and cripples," according to *The WPA Guide to 1930s New Jersey*. The chairs soon evolved into double chairs, then triple chairs.

Today, they may seem a dotty anachronism to a younger generation, but the wicker chairs transport thousands of tired-footed, nostalgic or just plain curious folks up and down the boardwalk every summer. The chairs actually operate year-round, generally until 1 a.m. Monday, Tuesday, and Wednesday; 2 a.m. Thursday and Sunday; 5 a.m. Friday and Saturday (the city requires the rolling chair companies to close at least two hours a day).

Taimanglo and his wife, Stephanie, own Ocean Rolling Chairs. Garry owns Boardwalk Rolling Chairs with James Lee, a local attorney who met Garry when the latter picked him up as an Uber fare. Garry owns 100 chairs, Taimanglo 50, and they sound both delighted and depressed about the life they have chosen. Garry is a blue-eyed, ruddy-faced guy in a flannel shirt, originally from Indiana, who in his early 20s moved east and became a trainer in New York City.

"I'd been reading about Atlantic City, I came down to check it out," he says. He ended up staying, getting a job as a trainer at Bally's. "One day on my break I went out to the boardwalk, saw the rolling chairs." He talked to one of the chair operators, found out he was making more than Garry. That was all Garry needed to apply for a job at Shore Rolling Chairs.

"I didn't look back," he says. "I was doing really well. The job was fun, the city was exciting." What did he like most about the job?

"The freedom, the exercise. I was in the best shape of my life when I operated the chairs." He worked at Shore Rolling Chairs seven years, then moved over to Atlantic City Rolling Chairs, owned by Larry Belfer, in 1995. Belfer is probably the most colorful character in Atlantic City rolling chair history. In 1984, Belfer, then a hotel clerk, bought 83 dilapidated chairs and launched Atlantic City Famous Rolling Chairs. "I was looking for a business venture and I got lucky," he said in a 1994 *New York Times* profile. "Everyone thought the days of rolling chairs were long gone."

The casino business—Resorts, the first one, opened in 1978—breathed new life into the rolling chair business. Gamblers used them to shuttle back and forth between casinos or just to take a break from craps table tension. Belfer ended up with 175 of the chairs. The chair operators, then and now, rented the chairs from their owners. One operator, Patrick Hamill, talked to the *Times* about several famous riders: "[Donald] Trump doesn't ride, but Marla [Maples, his second wife] always does because she can't walk on the boardwalk in high heels. Frank Sinatra used to come so much that they gave him his own chair."

In 1996, Garry started Boardwalk Rolling Chairs with his brother. In 2000, that company was sold; Garry moved to South Carolina for a year, returned and formed Royal Rolling Chairs. He and a partner ended up going to court. Garry won and was awarded 50 chairs, Jack Taimanglo the other 50. During that Uber ride, Lee asked Garry what he did for a living. He became so interested, he ended up investing in the company. In 2014, jitney trams started operating on the boardwalk. Chair operators were incensed. The tram fare was $3, and you could ride the entire boardwalk, compared to the $5 minimum rolling chair ride. Owners of the rolling chair companies filed a civil complaint against the city, but a judge refused to halt the trams' trial run. At the time, Jack Taimanglo called the city's decision to allow the trams "horrendous" and said, "The whole council should be arrested."

Later that year, the *Atlantic City Press* infuriated the chair owners even more. A November editorial said this:

> We mean no disrespect to these chair operators. They are often the newest immigrants to the city, doing what they can to get by. But this is no living for them . . . [the boardwalk] is lined with dozens of rolling chairs occupied by unkempt operators lazing away the day dozing, smoking and chatting with each other . . . as we said back in 2011, the rolling-chair business has become a classic example of Atlantic City shooting itself in the foot. It is time to pull the famous, iconic rolling chairs off the Boardwalk. They are doing the city's image more harm than good . . . the chairs have to go.

Ted Garry, co-owner of Boardwalk Rolling Chairs

Ouch.

Taimanglo and Garry are still in the business, but after listening to Garry list the fees and expenses, you wonder why. Every year, Boardwalk Rolling Chairs pays the city a total of $61,000 in fees for its 100 chairs. Potential operators must pay $40 for a background check, $45 for a drug test, and $85 for a city license before they can work the boardwalk. In the late '80s, maybe 75 percent of chair operators were Irish, according to Garry. Today, "there are a lot of Asians—Bangladesh, Pakistan. A lot of Haitians, Africans." His operators are required to wear a polo shirt and khaki or black pants; no T-shirts are allowed. One of his more veteran operators is 55-year-old Greg Stamm, a chair operator for the past 14 years. The Atlantic City native is quite familiar with the city entertainment scene; his parents operated the Hialeah Club for some 30 years. Stamm worked in the casinos, but it wasn't to his liking.

"I really didn't like that business," he says. "After a while, you realize you're just taking people's money."

He found the rolling chairs an ideal job—work outside, set your own hours. And he likes the late hours.

"Saturday night, I work until 5 a.m.," he explains. "Almost everyone else goes home at 1." His first night on the job, he made about $275. There was a Barry Manilow concert at one of the casinos and plenty of foot traffic on the boardwalk. Stamm's encyclopedic knowledge of AC restaurants—"I know every good restaurant in town"—and history makes him popular among passengers.

"I know every street in the city, even the old ones," he says. "Even the ones not here anymore, like St. Charles Avenue." Renting a chair costs about $175 a week in the summer, $125 for the rest of the year.

"Most guys do 8-, 10-, 12-hour shifts," he explains. "You have to make your own breaks, you gotta eat. Some guys go gambling."

The chairs just can't be parked anywhere. There are 20 "stand areas" on the boardwalk, most in front of casinos, where only one chair can park. Then there are "staging areas," next to the boardwalk rail, where chair operators wait for the stand area to clear. Fees are set—$5 for up to five blocks, $10 for 6–12 blocks, $15 for 13–21 blocks, $20 for 22–34 blocks. Most memorable day in rolling chair history as far as Garry is concerned: the day entertainer Ben Vereen proposed to a woman while riding one from Resorts to Caesars.

One day, all three Pointer Sisters rode, although Garry had no clue initially.

"I didn't know who they were," he says sheepishly. "I introduced myself—'I'm Ted.' They said, 'We're the Pointer Sisters.'"

Under the boardwalk, in Boardwalk Rolling Chairs' warehouse, Tenyo Yovchev is painting one of the chairs. Garry is painting and upgrading all his chairs. He says it will cost upward of $100,000. The upgrade will include LED signs and new tops. He makes the tops himself.

"I have a sewing machine; I do sew," he says, grinning.

A DAY AT THE TRAILER PARK

"DRAG $100 THROUGH A TRAILER park and there's no telling what you'll come up with," former Clinton advisor James Carville once famously said.

Now that we've gotten that trailer park joke out of the way—there will be only one or two more this chapter, I promise—let's start off with an apology to Dan Mandell, manager of Monmouth Mobile Home Park in South Brunswick, and the nice people who live there, because everyone in the business wants you to use the term *mobile home community* instead of *trailer park*.

But stereotypes die a slow death, and chances are, if you're driving past even the best-kept mobile home community, you're going to call it a trailer park. Mobile homes, says Mandell, "obviously work under a stigma."

I spent part of a rainy day at the mobile home community, and after talking to Mandell and getting to peek inside several homes, I was almost ready to buy a double-wide on the spot. The community's longtime owner was Art Roedel. He bought the 30-acre property for about $1 million in the '70s. The term *trailer park* "used to make Arthur very angry," Mandell said with a smile. "He would make it clear it wasn't trailer park but mobile home."

I did a story on the community's legendary Christmas tree nearly 20 years ago. "Mobile homes," Roedel told me then, "are filled with the most beautiful people."

The tree was a 40-foot pine with 63,101 lights (the iconic Rockefeller Center Christmas tree has a mere 30,000 or so lights). Monmouth Mobile Home Park's tree was a spectacular sight, more an apparition, glowing in the darkness along Route 1.

"That tree," Roedel told me, "is spiritual." In his later years, he lived in Princeton.

"They had a tree in town," Mandell says. "He used to hate on that tree so much. It was nothing like his." Roedel passed away in 2017, and the spectacularly lit tree has not been put up for eight, nine years.

"One of these days, we're going to bring back a real tree," Mandell promises.

The mobile home community was built in the 1950s and initially featured 47 homes on 40 acres. There are now 280 homes and 1,000 residents. If you think trailer parks—or mobile home communities—are a Southern or Midwest thing, you'd be wrong. An increasing number of Americans—most attracted by the affordable purchase price and rent—live in them. About 1.4 percent of Americans lived in mobile home communities in 1960; the number was

Sam Karbownik outside her mobile home at Monmouth Mobile Home Park

2.9 percent in 1970, 4.8 percent in 1980. and 6.75 percent in 1990. There are more in New Jersey than you might think. About 100,000 New Jerseyans live in the state's 170 mobile home communities.

Counties with the highest percentage of mobile homes: Cumberland (6.2), Salem (4.4), and Cape May (3.4), according to nj.com.

One of the state's most colorful mobile home communities was the Long Beach Island Trailer Park, a well-kept community of 146 mobile homes across the street from the ocean in well-to-do Holgate. It was run by Bob Muroff, a then 71-year-old surfer dude. I profiled the trailer park for the *Star-Ledger* in 2010; I still have the message from Muroff on my phone telling me how much he liked the story (reporters don't often get praised for their stories, trust me). The trailer park, alas, was destroyed by Hurricane Sandy in 2012.

Monmouth Mobile Home Park, meanwhile, seems destined to last forever. Mandell and his wife—Roedel's daughter—moved from Massachusetts seven years ago to run the community.

"It's been an interesting ride, a little bit of a roller coaster," he says. "A mobile home community is a microcosm of society. You get a little bit of everything.

"There's always something to do, someone always complaining about something," he adds. Complaints must be made in writing and presented to the landlord at the office during office hours. It's one of the rules and regulations at Monmouth Mobile Home Park. Others: No loud parties or excessive noise allowed at any time. Standard yard and patio furniture and approved storage sheds are the only items permitted outside units. All swimming pools are prohibited regardless of size. And so on. Most of Mandell's staff live here. "They all lived here before they worked here," he notes.

"A Community of Nice People" is how a brochure describes the community. There are bus trips to Atlantic City and Trenton Thunder games, Easter egg hunts, and carriage rides around Christmas. Amenities include a glass NBA backboard and a play set with 14 inches of "safety carpet." The community donates a stage to the town for concerts and in each of the past seven years has treated 25 needy kids to a shopping spree just before Christmas.

Nice things and nice people, unfortunately, never appear in Hollywood movies about trailer parks. The British daily newspaper the *Guardian* came up with a list of notable trailer park movies. They included *The Wrestler* ("nothing signifies 'down on his luck all-American' like a trailer home"); *8 Mile* ("Eminem's early rendition of 'I live at home in a trailer' to the tune of Sweet Home Alabama was not a promising start . . ."); *No Country for Old Men* ("Basically, you can blame the trailer home for the whole sorry affair here"); and *Pink Flamingos* ("The leering, manky-toothed granddaddy of trailer park movies, John Waters's gleeful shocker firmly established the trailer park as the repository of all things debauched and trashy"). You, much less my publisher, would not want me to list those debauched and trashy things.

Stereotypes aside, trailer park living is not for everyone. Claustrophobic? You might want to look elsewhere; the units are often separated by mere feet. You raise your voice even a smidge, your next-door neighbor will hear it.

How much does trailer park living cost? Older homes at Monmouth Mobile Home Park cost about $20,000; new ones $50,000–80,000. The fixed monthly fee is $730, which includes water, sewer, property taxes, garbage, and recycling. The units are usually 16 × 60, about 1,000 square feet.

Barb Henrickson has lived here a mere "47 or 48 years." Her husband, Jack, has lived here for 36 years. She had been renting a home in Long Valley when a friend recommended mobile homes. She had never heard of the term. Barb bought a brand-new house at Monmouth Mobile Home Park for $10,000 seven weeks later, a double-wide. Her first monthly rent was

$108. "It's affordable, you have a nice piece of property," she says. Several of her friends "are still struggling, paying off their house or paying condo fees," she adds.

"I like going out and planting flowers, I like growing tomatoes. We like to sit out on the deck. We have everything you'd have in the house, you just don't have property."

Sam Karbownik's parents moved in here in 1972. Her sister Natalie has lived here since she was born. Sam calls the community "very comfortable, very community-oriented, very safe." She and her husband bought their unit for $12,000 in 2014. It's a 12 × 65 Schult with two bedrooms, a spacious eat-in kitchen, living room, and a bathroom with a Jacuzzi tub. Schult is one of the leading mobile home builders.

"There's no reason to move out of here; it's one of the more affordable places to live in town," she says. "It's become a very realistic way of living."

A NIGHT AT THE FOOD TRUCK

SO YOU WANT TO START your own food truck? Walk away from the dreary 9–5 and be your own boss? Listen to Marcus Crawford run down the expenses *after* he bought a food truck off Craigslist.

"Two fridges and a grill, $1,300. Steam table, $350. Stainless steel walls, $1,400. Hood, $400. Fire suppression system, $1,400. Wrap, $3,500. Propane box, $800. Window, $1,700. Generator, $3,200." That doesn't include the $6,000 or so he spent on engine and transmission repairs after he put his Bro-Ritos truck on the road.

Still want to start your own food truck?

Bro-Ritos is, as of this writing, the state's only specialty burrito food truck. There are a dozen or more taco trucks roaming the New Jersey food landscape, but no burrito trucks.

Disclaimer: I love food trucks. I have written about them at length for nj.com and have served as a judge at the Jersey Shore Food Truck Festival at Monmouth Park, the state's largest ongoing food truck event, for the past six years. And yes, I've entertained dreams about operating my own food truck. Not sure what I'd serve. But after listening to Crawford detail the expenses and various headaches involving his truck (everything's running smoothly now), I may rethink that dream.

Marcus is a 2005 graduate of Old Bridge High School who received a BA from Florida International. He and Jonathan Gibbs, who attended high school with Marcus's brother, teamed up to run a SoupMan truck, a familiar sight in downtown Newark. But they wanted their own truck, to be their own boss. "We were either going to do a chicken wing or burrito concept," Marcus explains. "But every wing truck we've seen didn't have longevity. And there was no burrito truck. Taco trucks, but no burrito trucks."

They needed a truck and a catchy name. They bought the truck on Craigslist for $8,000. They could have bought a new truck from someone like Custom Mobile Food Equipment in Hammonton, but that would have cost $50,000–$100,000. For names, they kicked around Brothers Burritos and Burritos Brothers, then Dan DeMiglio, owner of Callahan's Hot Dogs in Norwood, said why not join the two words—Bro-Ritos!

Chipotle, the fast-food chain, was an inspiration for Bro-Ritos—how food is ordered, station-to-station. "You only have so much time to make your money," Marcus says. "The faster you get the food out, the better."

Bro-Ritos made its debut at a PBA-sponsored food truck event at Lurker Park in East Hanover in 2016.

"That was a good event until we tried to leave and the truck wouldn't start," Jonathan recalls. That was the beginning of a series of mechanical issues with the truck.

"This truck has broke down so many times," Jon says dispiritedly.

"Obviously, we were frustrated," Marcus adds. "We learned not to dwell on the little nuances, not to let them get us down. Why stress it? Try to be a stress-free as possible."

"Giving up," he adds, "is not an option." 2016 was "a loss" financially, but nevertheless, it was an improvement over the SoupMan truck. The Bro-Ritos truck has appeared at graduation parties, baby showers, engagement parties, corporate headquarters, bar mitzvahs, weddings, and other events from Ringwood to Avalon.

The best parties, according to Jonathan, "are where alcohol is involved. It's fun when they drink . . . they're superfriendly."

He and Jonathan work about 200 days a year. "I wish it was closer to 300 or 365, but the weather just eats us up," Marcus explains. I caught up with them at the Ranney School in Tinton Falls. The Bro-Ritos truck was parked outside the gym; there was a basketball game inside. When the truck opened for business at 4, a line quickly formed.

The most popular item on the truck is the Big Fella Bro, with chicken, beef, and sweet peppers. It's quite a handful. You can also get a Chicken Chipotle Bro, pulled chicken with sautéed onions, roasted peppers, and a "special chipotle blend"; a Black Beans Bro, with rice, beans, and adobo; tacos; and quesadillas. The colorful wrap encircling the truck shows Marcus, Jonathan, and Jarid Thomas, Marcus's cousin. They searched for an artist to design the wrap and, on Instagram, came across a Brazilian artist named Rafael Dukenny. After trading emails and suggestions for three months, they had a design and had the wrap done in Lakewood.

"We did it lime green," Marcus explains. "No other truck is this color. And green because New Jersey is the Garden State."

Marcus admits he has no culinary background. So how did he learn? "I went to a few family and friends, asked them to teach me."

BLUE-RAP (Black and Latino Urban Entrepreneurship–Retail Acceleration Program), a 13-week program offered by the Rutgers University Center for Urban Entrepreneurship and Economic Development, Marcus says, "helped us get a complete understanding of the importance of keeping our books and our finances in order. We now know that a company's financials tell a story and that it's the most important part of a business. We use what we learned in BLUE-RAP daily in the operation of Bro-Ritos."

In 2018, they won two awards, for best new business and young entrepreneurs, in the NJ Black Businesses' annual NJBB Best in Black Business Awards. Marcus and Jonathan will

Jonathan Gibbs (on the grill) and Jarid Thomas inside the Bro-Ritos food truck

have a second truck on the road, plus a storefront, in 2020. Possible storefront locations: Newark, Jersey City, Harrison, Bloomfield, Montclair. "We're open to New Brunswick—anywhere where there's foot traffic," Jonathan explains. "We're trying to build a brand, we're trying to do what we're good at, instead of trying to do too much," Marcus says.

There's a system inside the truck. Marcus, stationed at the window, takes the orders and fills the burritos. Jonathan heats up the tortillas, weighing down the tortilla press with a box of food handler vinyl gloves, and adds such toppings as lettuce and cheese to the burritos. He also makes the quesadillas. Jarid, manning the pickup window, rings up the orders, adding the totals on a smartphone. Movements are economical; it's food truck choreography in tight quarters.

"What can I get for you, buddy?" Marcus asks a youthful customer.

"Chicken chipotle."

"What kind of toppings?"

"Lettuce and cheese."

"Lettuce and cheese? Can you slide to the front window for me?"

The Bro-Ritos soundtrack tonight—there's a boom box in the corner—includes "For K. K." by Zeke Mar Lee, then "Paramedic" by SOB x RBE and "Unfair" from 6LACK.

A teenage girl sidles up to a male friend at the counter: "Buy me a quesadilla; I'll pay you back," she says.

My Favorite NJ Food Trucks (Apart from Bro-Ritos, of course)

Let me preface this list by saying that I love pretty much all the Jersey food trucks out there. It was nearly impossible to narrow it down to 30. Hopefully, no hard feelings from those left off this list! Note: most food trucks move around to different locations; check their websites, Facebook pages, or Twitter feeds for the latest info.

Amanda Bananas. A truck that revolves around bananas? That's Amanda Bananas, which creates banana-based frozen desserts—banana cream pie, Almond Joy, piña colada, and more. They're often at the Jersey Shore Food Truck Festival and Trucktoberfest, both at Monmouth Park. I once described the banana cream pie as "a cool pillowy pleasure on a plate." Maybe I got carried away a bit. But it's so good.

Amazing Taste. Joshua Muhammad, owner of Amazing Taste, bought his truck for $15,000 on Craigslist and opened it in Plainfield, where he grew up. He now has a storefront on Route 22 in North Plainfield. The menu is a mix of soul food, Caribbean, and Latino dishes. Try the jerk chicken; it's spicier than the version you'll find at most Caribbean restaurants.

Aroy-D, the Thai Elephant. Jon Hepner, owner of the Thai Elephant truck, is one of the pioneers of the Jersey food truck scene; he helped found the New Jersey Food Truck Association. He and his wife, Pupay, operate the truck, a converted Matco Tools truck. Aroy-D is Thai for "very yummy." All the Thai standards are here—pad thai, pad king, chicken satay, mango and sticky rice, and more. There is also a storefront in Verona.

Cheezen. The best food truck grilled cheese? At Cheezen, which offers them in ways "that make you smile." There's the Traditional, with American cheese and bacon on country sourdough; a pork roll grilled cheese; a mac and cheese grilled cheese; and a prosciutto Caprese, with mozzarella and Gruyere over thinly sliced prosciutto *de parma*, Jersey tomatoes, and basil pesto.

Dark Side of the Moo. Easily the state's most adventurous food truck, Dark Side of the Moo goes where no other truck dares to go—yak, camel, and bison burgers; wild boar tacos; smoked alligator with *picante* sauce. When I last saw owner Tyrone Green, he was talking about introducing a guinea pig burger. Green left his job at a Canadian bank in 2009 to start his truck. There is also a storefront in Jersey City.

El Lechon de Negron. The truck, which specializes in authentic Puerto Rican pig roast and cuisine, rolled out in 2012. They always seem to win an award at the Jersey Shore Food Truck Festival at Monmouth Park. The *pernil* (slow-roasted pork shoulder marinated in a homemade mojo sauce) and *chimichurri* chicken are musts. There is also a storefront in Union.

Empanada Guy. Carlos Serrano rules over an empanada empire—a storefront in Freehold, plus trucks in Morris Plains, Bradley Beach, and Woodbridge (trucks in Old Bridge and South Brunswick are relocating as of this writing). The former Elizabeth High School baseball player competed on Lifetime's *Supermarket Superstar* show several years ago. He didn't win, but his competitiveness and drive remain intact. Look for the bright-red truck and the guy with the red bandanna and red shoes.

Empanada Lady. Empanada Guy has worthy competition in the Empanada Lady. Her empanadas might be the fattest ones out there—thick, bulbous, crunchy creations. There are 19 varieties; my favorites are Indian samosa and chicken and potatoes. The cheery storefront in Verona is decorated with Caribbean travel posters.

Empanada Monster. You can never have enough empanada trucks. "Colombia's delicious food in a food truck" is the slogan at Empanada Monster. The yellow truck offers "monster empanadas," plus sweet plantains, fried cassava, Colombian breads, flan, and more.

Falafull. "Arabian bites, American dreams" is the slogan of this bright-green food truck. Falafel is available as a sandwich, plate, or tacos, the latter topped with cabbage salad and a fiery sauce. There's hummus, tahini, baba ghanoush, a Bang Bang Chicken Sandwich (a pita stuffed with chicken, lettuce, tomato, and garlic tahini sauce), and don't forget the fries.

Fired Up Flatbread. From compliance officer in a financial firm to food truck operator: Isn't that how everyone makes a career move? Marc Viscomi decided the compliance officer gig just wasn't him; after all, he had graduated from the French Culinary Institute and had served as executive chef at acclaimed Dylan Prime in New York City. He found a former Snap-On Tools truck in Vermont, spent $70,000 retrofitting it, and opened his Fired Up Flatbread pizza truck in May 2014 at the Flemington Farmer's Market. The truck can be found at festivals and farmers' markets.

The Flying Pie Guy. Mike Peacock is the Flying Pie Guy. These are not fruit pies but savory pies filled with beef, pork, onions, carrots, peas, and other fillings. There's even a veggie option, a curried garden pie. I love his Angus steak and Guinness pie. The truck's name is a tribute to William Francis King, a pie seller in mid-1800s Sydney also known for his amazing athletic feats; he once walked 1,634 miles in 39 days.

Freezy Freeze. Andrew Deming doesn't just make ice cream; he puts on a show while doing it. He makes liquid nitrogen ice cream, the ice-cold mist rising from the counter like from some mad scientist movie.

Five Sisters Catering. There really are five sisters, although only three of them actively work on the Five Sisters truck, owned by their dad, George, and mom, Libby. There's Ashley, Hailey, and Summer, with Savannah and Piper waiting in the wings. The truck hit the big time when it was voted the nation's best burger food truck by Mobile Cuisine. The menu includes whiskey tango, brie, and smokehouse sliders, and several fat sandwiches, including the Philly (cheesesteak, chicken fingers, mozzarella sticks, thick-cut fries, ketchup, and mayo, all on a hoagie).

Fork in the Road. Duck confit on a food truck? Must be Scott Cullen and his Fork in the Road truck. The duck confit sandwich is a supremely satisfying blend of duck bacon, duck liver mousse, brie, blackberry *gastrique*, pickled shallots, and greens on thin-stretched focaccia. He also does a chipotle skirt steak *torta*, braised short rib, a portabella and oyster mushroom sandwich, and herbed truffle fries, among other dishes.

Good Food = Good Mood. Now that's a great name for a food truck. It's run by Dean Hodecker and his sister, Emily. Their mood-altering menu includes burgers, crispy mac 'n' cheese, avocado fries, parmesan rice balls, tacos, and honey mustard bacon fries.

IncrediBalls. A mainstay of the Jersey City food truck scene, IncrediBalls offers heaping meatball sandwiches spanning the meatball world—the Southern Smoked Pork; the Swedish (beef and pork meatballs with brown gravy and a sour cream dill spread); the Barbecue Pork; the Jamaican Jerk Chicken; the Vegetarian (black bean and quinoa with sushi rice and chili aioli); and the banh mi spicy pork meatball with pickled carrots, jalapeños, and sriracha slaw.

Johnny's Pork Roll. You want to call it Taylor ham instead of pork roll? Take it up with Johnny Yarusi, owner of Johnny's Pork Roll. The Sandwich is a classic, near-perfect pork roll, egg, and cheese sandwich. There's also the Western, with provolone and sautéed peppers and onions; the Pulled Pork Roll, with sweet BBQ and Asian lime slaw; and the PBLT, with bacon, lettuce, and tomato. There's also a storefront in Red Bank.

Juanito Lunch Truck, Marsh Street, Port Newark. There's a lot of good cheap eats in Port Newark / Port Elizabeth. Hey, all those truckers carrying goods to the port have to eat somewhere. Juanito is one of my two or three favorite trucks there. The chicken stew (*pollo guisado*) and pork stew are hearty, savory successes.

LaLa's Puerto Rican Kitchen, Old Bridge. A lady named LaLa and a former male stripper are the duo behind this truck. Lisa Cartagena—she acquired the nickname "Lala" as a kid—has come a long way from selling empanadas at a tiki bar on a paintball field. Her specialties now include pernil (roast pork), *arroz con gandules* (rice and pigeon peas), empanadas, and *alcapurrias* (beef-filled fritters). The former stripper? That would be her husband, Frank Mojica, who helps her on the truck.

Lexylicious. New Jersey's "first and best ice cream sandwich truck" started with then 17-year-old Alexa Hesse making Fruity Pebbles ice cream sandwiches at home in April 2015. Her first public appearance, in a tent at a Toms River street festival, was such a hit that a truck soon followed. And then a storefront in Point Pleasant Beach. You can customize your ice cream sandwich by selecting the outside (cookies, pretzels, potato chips, etc.) and inside (vanilla, chocolate, strawberry, etc.).

Luigi's Ice Cream. Luigi Beltran, owner of Luigi's Ice Cream truck, a familiar sight in Jersey City, ratcheted up his ice cream game by opening the state's first "ice cream speakeasy" inside Ani Ramen in Jersey City. He offers boozy—alcoholic-infused—ice cream, and yes, you will have to show ID. Flavors include Patrón XO Cafe and chocolate chip ice cream; Godiva Dark Chocolate Liqueur and fudge brownie ice cream; and my favorite, Hennessy and pineapple ice cream.

Mexi Flip Taco Truck. This truck really gets around. One summer found them working Jersey City, West Orange, New Brunswick, Tuckerton, New Egypt, and Sewell (Gloucester County). Good tacos, especially the steak, pork, and mango chicken varieties.

Oink and Moo BBQ. Josh Sacks spent several years as a barbecue vagabond, roaming the country in search of the best BBQ techniques. He opened his Oink and Moo BBQ truck in 2012;

another truck came along in 2014, with a third truck and a storefront in Florham Park added in 2015. In 2015, Oink and Moo placed sixth on Daily Meal's ranking of the 101 Best Food Trucks in America.

The Outslider. Bob Leahy lost his job due to Hurricane Sandy and vowed "to work in a place that was immune to the will of hurricanes." That's how The Outslider started. His burgers aren't just lettuce-topped mini–beef burgers; you can get a beer-battered haddock slider, a chicken breast slider, a bourbon BBQ slider, and an Asian Chix slider with grilled chicken and a spicy teriyaki glaze.

Pizza Vita. Why aren't there more pizza food trucks? Got me. You can always get a good pie at the Pizza Vita truck (there's a sister restaurant in Summit). In the warmer months, it's on the road nearly seven days a week around the state. Pizzas come out hot and fast (60 to 90 seconds) in the Italian wood-fired pizza oven. They include the Regina (crushed and cherry tomatoes, *bufala* mozzarella, basil), *margherita* (crushed tomatoes, fresh homemade mozzarella, basil), and a white pie with regular and *bufala* mozzarella.

Rodgers Real BBQ, Avenel. For good barbecue, head to the jail. Todd Rodgers's Rodgers Real BBQ truck is parked right across the street from East Jersey (formerly Rahway) State Prison in Woodbridge. He's cooked at Stage Left and the Molly Pitcher Inn and says he's a "crazy man" in the kitchen. Try his ribs, half chicken, or barbecue turkey sandwich; make sure you get a heap of coleslaw atop the latter, which turns it into a monstrous, marvelous mess.

Tacos Al Carbon, Peach Street, Hammonton. One of a handful of trucks on this list with a fixed location, Tacos Al Carbon serves cheap, tasty tacos. The *tortas* are huge, stuffed with meat, tomatoes, avocados, and more.

Top Shelf Mobile Cuisine. The best food truck dish I had all last year was the grilled lamb chops at Top Shelf Mobile Cuisine. Perfectly grilled (medium rare, of course) and bursting with flavor, they were proof you can get standout food on a truck. The salad of feta, cucumbers, and kalamatas (three of my favorite things!) made for a superior side.

Waffle de Lys. Waffle de Lys offers Belgian waffles with a French twist; most of the toppings are made with ingredients imported from Belgium and France. The waffles, with caramelized pearl sugar, are known in Belgium as Liege waffles. Toppings include Belgian chocolate, salted caramel, raspberry coulis (my favorite!), Nutella, and fresh strawberries. Savory waffles include BBQ pulled pork, smoked salmon and chives, and tomato and mozzarella.

IF YOU ARE ONE OF those unlikable folks who don't like Mother Goose for whatever reason, you might want to proceed to the next chapter.

The Mother in question, splendid in a purple gown and white ruffled sleeves and sporting a kindly grin, greets visitors to Storybook Land on Route 40 in Egg Harbor Township. I have a dim memory of going here as a kid. Maybe I never did, who knows. In any event, the amusement park remains a draw, attracting 60,000–80,000 visitors a year.

Somehow, in a world of Great Adventure, high-tech rides, video games, and other distractions, New Jersey's old-school amusement parks survive, if not thrive. The Land of Make Believe, in Hope, opened in 1954. Wild West City, the western heritage theme park, opened in 1957. It's not an amusement park, but Space Farms in Beemerville does have 500-plus live animals, nine museum buildings, antique cars and firearms, and more. All four attractions are proof that you don't need high tech to create hijinks for kids of all ages. Storybook Land, built around nursery rhyme characters, opened one year after the Land of Make Believe in 1955. Chief made it possible.

That was John Fricano's nickname. He was a house painter; his wife, Esther, worked as a secretary on a poultry farm. "[They] had a vision to create attractions that depict the familiar nursery rhymes and fairy tales that have, to this day, remained timeless and relevant even in today's world of Minecraft and SpongeBob," according to a story in the New Jersey Amusement Association's 2015 Directory (the NJAA honored Storybook Land in 2015).

The Fricanos bought five acres on Route 40 to tap into Atlantic City–bound traffic and to cash in on a sudden and dramatic American desire in the 1950s to hit the road and see the country.

"The highway system was put in place, people got in their cars and looked for places to visit," says Jessica Fricano, the couple's granddaughter and one of the park's current owners. "On the way to the Shore, there was nothing to do." And before the Atlantic City Expressway opened in 1964, Route 30 and Route 40 were the main direct routes to the Shore from South Jersey and Philly.

Chief cleared the land with just a few hand tools, a pickup truck, and a homemade crane fashioned from telephone poles. "More than once," Fricano was pulled over and issued tickets by police for overloading his pickup truck while hauling gravel for the park's walkways,

The teapot snack bar at Storybook Land

according to the NJAA account. Esther and John "would find things by the side of the road" to accessorize their park, according to Jessica. They'd pick up rides or equipment from parks that went out of business. Mother Goose came from a defunct park in Maryland.

Storybook Land opened Easter Sunday, April 10, 1955. The first attraction was the Little Red Schoolhouse. Admission: 75 cents (it's now $24.50 online and $27.50 at the door; admission includes unlimited rides). Esther made curtains, tablecloths, and costumes for the animated characters and would dress up as Mother Goose. She was also Storybook Land's first chef; her Humpty Dumpty sundaes were popular. Another early attraction was the old chapel from a Vineland farm. The first ride came along in the early 1960s: the Jolly Trolley, fashioned from an old Fiat car.

Today, there are 41 attractions, from Humpty Dumpty, Hickory Dickory Dock, and the Three Little Pigs to Cinderella's Pumpkin Coach, Old Mother Hubbard, and the Three Bears' House. The 17 rides include the Whirly Bug, Zip Zap Racers, J&J Railroad, and Tick-Tock Clock Drop. The most popular nonride is the tunnel, which tells the story of Alice in Wonderland in trippy '60s-psychedelic fashion (or maybe it seemed that way because I was having '60s flashbacks, especially with the White Rabbit). The most popular ride: Bubbles the Coaster, in the shape of a friendly sea dragon, which climbs a 15-foot hill before sending passengers through a sea of bubbles.

The train that winds its way through the park was bought from the village of Smithville and made its debut in 1996. The Three Bears, Little Red Riding Hood, and Snow White's House have been updated with animatronics—talking characters.

"People say we're old school, but we keep up with the times," Jessica Fricano says. "But it's low key, it's not sensory overload. You don't have games dinging." A real caboose, from the Lehigh & Hudson River Railway, serves as the Caboose Café. Chief added a lighthouse because he lived in one when he was in the Coast Guard.

Another popular attraction is Billy Goats Gruff, where kids can put feed into a bucket attached to a pulley to feed the goats atop a tower. The park opens Palm Sunday weekend and closes December 30. But over the winter, there's plenty of work to do.

"We take everything apart and put it back together," Jessica explains. "Our rides get their yearly maintenance and tests."

There are 15–20 full-time employees, 100 or so seasonal. The busiest month is not in the summer; it's December because of the spectacular holiday light display—one-million-plus lights that turn Storybook Land into a wired winsome wonderland. In mid-November, the lights are turned on for the first time. Santa appears in his chimney, waves his magic wand, and those million-plus lights dazzle the sky.

"We get people all over coming," Jessica says. "It's amazing, it's magical. It's not just families; it's a date night. You get a hot chocolate, go on the ride. It's the atmosphere; everyone's in a good mood."

During the year, there are classic car shows, a pirate adventure day, and a princess tea party, among other events. Mother Goose and the Three Little Bears are great, but even old-school gets stale if you don't keep things fresh.

Jessica has worked here full time since graduating from Stockton in 2010, although she worked in the snack bar when she was 14. She says her dad and his sister are the park's "head honchos," while she and her brother are "the honchos in training." Storybook Land is "one of the few parks that allow you to bring food, a cooler in," she notes. "And parking's free."

There's a Story Land in Glen, NH, and a Storybook Land in Aberdeen, ND. "Follow the Yellow Brick Road to a land of enchantment which includes more than 65 larger-than-life nursery rhyme themed exhibits," reads a description of the latter. "Visit a medieval castle, complete with moat and guarded by knights in armor. See Rapunzel with her hair let down over the castle wall waiting for her prince to arrive . . ."

I've seen photos of the North Dakota Storybook Land. It's no match for New Jersey's version.

"We don't have Six Flags or Hershey's or Disney numbers," Jessica says. "We're not a big park." No matter. The old-school amusement park endures. Nursery rhymes are still viable in the age of Minecraft.

John Fricano passed away in 2009, Esther in 2015. The head honchos and honchos in training are keeping the magical park on Route 40 alive.

INSIDE THE TRAFFIC MANAGEMENT CENTER

THE DARKENED CONTROL ROOM MIGHT remind you of a ballroom, minus the white table-cloths and baked chicken. Dozens of desks, all with four to five monitors, rise slightly from the front of the room, where dispatchers sit, to the back, where supervisors are stationed. A giant screen, 55 feet wide, is filled with smaller screens, all showing traffic on the Garden State Parkway, New Jersey Turnpike, and various state and federal highways—Routes 1/9, 37, 70, 287, 295, and 495, among others.

A state map in the center of the big screen shows all the major highways, color-coded. Sections of highways marked in green means traffic is flowing. Yellow: moderate delays. Orange: congestion. Red: standstill. Black: the road is closed. The parkway southbound, which I'll negotiate in an hour or so, is green, green, green all the way home. For the time being anyway. Those who work in the Traffic Management Center know that everything can change in an instant. Above and behind me is the center's "situation room."

"That's where the governor goes whenever there's something going on," Ruth Rodriguez explains. The Newark resident, who started as a dispatcher here 15 years ago, is now manager of the Traffic Management Center in Woodbridge, just down the road from a Wawa.

"I am responsible for this whole building and everything that happens," Rodriguez says. "Everything from traffic management to staffing to outside agency support."

It's 5:19 p.m., and her usual shift is 7–3. So why is she here? "Stuff happens," she says, smiling.

"Stuff happens" is as good a way as any to describe the ebb and flow and freneticism on major New Jersey highways, particularly the Garden State Parkway, the road every Jerseyan loves to hate. The turnpike doesn't get quite the same hate, mostly because it carries much less traffic—260 million vehicles annually compared to the parkway's annual 470 million. That's about 1.2 million vehicles a day on the parkway, about 700,000 vehicles a day on the turnpike. Neither road is a picnic any time of the day or year. I don't believe actual picnics have ever been held on either roadway (not really a smart idea), but everything else has. In one of the more spectacular incidents ever on either highway, 30 railcars ended up on the turnpike by Exit 13 after Hurricane Sandy.

"We've had small planes land on both highways," Rodriguez notes. "We've had overturned trucks with porta potties. Overturned armored trucks. We've had chickens on the road. Turkeys. Anything and everything comes through here." On those desktop monitors, incidents are inputted by categories—accidents with injuries, brush fire, cargo spill, delays, debris spill, disabled truck, disabled vehicles, and so on.

The 55-foot screen reminded me of the big board at North American Aerospace Defense Command headquarters inside Cheyenne Mountain, Colorado, which I visited about 25 years ago for a story. The main difference, of course, is that the former monitors incidents on two of the world's busiest highways, and the latter watches for nuclear missiles. The Cheyenne Mountain complex now serves as NORAD's alternate command center.

The Traffic Management Center is also staffed by New Jersey State Police (to the left) and the state Department of Transportation (to the right). The privately funded New Jersey Turnpike Authority (which covers the parkway and turnpike) pays the salaries of troopers who work on the parkway and turnpike. There are three state police stations on the turnpike (Cranbury, Moorestown, Newark) and three on the parkway (Holmdel, Bloomfield, Galloway), plus two parkway substations (Pleasant Plains, Avalon).

There are six New Jersey Turnpike Authority dispatchers for each 10- or 12-hour day shift; there are four dispatchers overnight. In the summer, they average about 400 calls a day; during a snowstorm, the number might be 2,000–3,000 daily.

"Blizzard of '96, I was in here three days," recalls Kerry Covey, another shift supervisor. "One of the guys would go out and get pizza, Subway." A bag of Popeye's chicken tenders and a supersized Pepsi are on his desk; it's what's for dinner.

A total of 52 tow companies work the two highways. The "northern mixing bowl," in Ridgefield Park, is where the turnpike eastern and western spurs split, going southbound. The "southern mixing bowl," in Newark, is where the turnpike eastern and western spurs split, going northbound. The ramp from the turnpike to Route 80 is called "tanker turn" because of the propensity of trucks to tip over. My two visits to the Traffic Management Center definitely added to my Jersey highway vocabulary.

On the second visit, Robert Strauss sat at one of the shift-supervisor stations.

"Sometimes you just want to put up a sign—hey stupid, slow down," he says, shaking his head. No one in his or her right mind heads southbound on the parkway on a Friday summer afternoon; staffers here have seen more Shore-bound motorists leave on Thursday and return on Monday to avoid the epic traffic snarls on Friday afternoon southbound and Sunday afternoon northbound. Supervisors can quickly punch in warnings—"Crash ahead: be prepared to stop" or "Delays ahead: be prepared to stop" or "Reduce speed: congestion ahead." If you call 511, you get info the supervisors inputted.

Strauss dials 511, and gets this message: "On the Garden State Parkway there are six incidents as of 4:42."

"That's what I just put in," he says.

Monitors (and dinner) at the supervisor's desk, Traffic Management Center, Woodbridge

There are 173 cameras on the turnpike, 139 on the parkway. All can be switched on in the Traffic Management Center. The Amber in Amber Alert, in case you didn't know (I didn't), stands for America's Missing Broadcast Emergency Response.

"I take [this job] very seriously because I know we affect millions of people," Rodriguez says. "We can make a difference [in them] getting home to their family. We affect millions of people. We have to be careful with the decisions we make. Nobody knows about us, but we affect so many people."

On my first visit, she played a tape that is played when staffers "need a laugh." It's a man drunk, drugged, or disturbed—or maybe all three.

"I'm going northbound but also heading south," he begins. "I'm perplexed."

"Northbound on the turnpike?" the dispatcher asks.

"Yes."

"You sure you're not going southbound?"

"I am going southbound."

He is asked how clearly he can see the sign. "I can see it as clearly as . . ." and then adds a vulgar reference I can't print here. Lesson to be learned here: All calls to the center are taped. Don't say anything you may regret later.

"You never know what's going to be on the other end of the line," Rodriguez says. "We [once] had a woman [motorist call in]. We heard her just before she got hit by a truck. It was literally her last breath."

WHERE 600,000 INSECTS ARE ON THE MENU

IS THERE ANYTHING ON EARTH uglier than a vulture? Tiny heads, crinkly beaks, and no voice boxes, which means they hiss and rasp a lot. And let's not get started on their predilection for carcasses. But I am about to learn something about vultures that makes me reconsider my abysmally low opinion of these noxious birds of prey.

"They are very curious," Chris Soucy says as we stand outside an outdoor enclosure at the Raptor Trust. "When our staff goes in there to clean up the cages, they'll come and pull peoples' shoelaces, nibble on your ankles. They're kind of like the class clowns."

Who knew? But let's not forget that vultures are among the stinkiest birds, mostly when they throw up—a sight I don't want to treat myself to.

"They're nature's garbage cans," Soucy continues. "These guys have large wings because they need to soar to find the dead stuff."

There are two turkey vultures and one black vulture in the outdoor enclosures at the Raptor Trust, a wild bird rehabilitation center in Millington that Soucy's dad, Len, started in the late 1970s. It's located just outside the Great Swamp National Wildlife Refuge; the Environmental Education Center in Lord Stirling Park is just down the road.

The Raptor Trust takes in about 6,000 birds a year, a staggering number when you consider the compact if not cramped space Soucy and staff work in. The infirmary is where the action is.

"There may be hundreds and hundreds of birds here," Soucy explains. "Last year we had 670 birds here at one time. They were all chattering because they were hungry."

"This room is for baby baby baby birds," he says, as we wind our way through the building. One item on a shelf: extra-large Wee-Wee pads.

There's an injured duck in a cage—"somebody found it on their driveway in Lincoln Park," according to Soucy. "We already have a home for him," says Alyssa Frediani, part of the rehab staff.

The center maintains a big red notebook of contacts—people willing to take in birds. The admitting office is open 24 hours a day year-round; you can leave an injured bird anytime.

"Their nest got chopped down or they flew into a glass building or they got shot or poisoned," explains Soucy when asked how birds get injured. "They didn't do that; [humans] did. In the spring we get a lot of orphans. They're not injured—their nest fell down. Mama got run

Chris Soucy with a barred owl at the Raptor Trust

over by a car. They don't need surgery; they need food." The peak admit time is May, June, and July. As of November 20, 2019, 4,214 birds had been admitted.

One reason for the high number of admits in recent years: the ease of reporting an injured bird on your smartphone.

"If you found an injured hawk 15 years ago, you would probably call the police or a vet. Now it's a one-step process with your smartphone." There are 11 licensed bird rehabbers in New Jersey, with the Raptor Trust the best known.

Despite the name, raptors—hawks, eagles, falcons, ospreys, owls—make only about 10 percent of birds admitted at the Raptor Trust. The most common birds admitted in 2018 were, in order, American robins, mourning doves, mallard ducks, blue jays, and common grackles. In 2018, there were 6,002 admits (a record) and 168 species; 2,407 birds were released back into the wild.

The outdoor enclosures, which can be visited by the public, hold 50–55 birds, all "permanently crippled," Soucy says. "They can't be released back into the woods. Anything that can be released into the wild, is. We make the choice for them. If we left all these cages open, every single one would leave and die in the swamp. They don't want to be here. They're not pets; they're wild animals." He smiles. "They have medical care, great health insurance, food from the cafeteria—it's a good gig."

The Raptor Trust started not with birds but with dogs. In the late 1950s, Len and Diane Soucy—they had met in a bowling alley—had been breeding Shetland sheepdogs for show. On a summer day in 1960, they visited a dog breeder in Livingston. There Diane saw her first white-breasted nuthatch—"a spunky little bird that has an unusual ability to climb not only straight up a tree but straight down as well," according to an account in the Raptor Trust's 2016 annual report.

"She asked for a bird feeder"—Chris Soucy's arms take in the property—"now look." His parents bought five woodsy acres in Millington, part of Long Hill Township, Morris County. Chris was four years old when his parents moved here. "There was no such thing as wildlife rehabilitation at the time."

Asked for childhood memories of the place, he replies, "Waking up early to clean out the bird poop."

In the 1960s, according to Soucy, it was legal to hunt raptors. "The prevailing attitude was these birds were pests—we're going to eat your chickens or carry your children away." In the late 1970s, the New Jersey Raptor Association was formed; it was later renamed the Raptor Trust and incorporated as a nonprofit. Len would laughingly call it "this great mess" he had gotten his family and friends into.

Len Soucy passed away in 2014 at the age of 82. "An extraordinary man who made a major impact on both the wildlife of New Jersey and the attitudes of people living with wildlife," read a memorial in the *Daily Record*.

"Who would do this in their backyard?" Chris Soucy asks. "He and my mom gave up every possible path to normalcy to choose this." He calls his mom "the internal hard drive of the organization"—she can recall when a donor went active and other minutiae. When his dad passed, the Raptor Trust's board asked Chris to take over.

"They asked me first. I could have said no. I would have been a jerk to say no." He proudly shows off a state-of-the-art mobile medical laboratory, stocked with digital radiology and digital endoscopy equipment, a modern anesthesia unit, and a Doppler blood pressure monitor, among other features.

"Brand new everything," Soucy says. "It enables our staff to work with sterile tools." Handouts at the center tell you everything you'd want to know about raptors. It won't take long before you know the difference between buteos (robust hawks with long, broad, rounded wings and short, broad tails) and accipiters (hawks with short, rounded wings and long, rudder-like tails that inhabit deeply wooded areas).

Soucy is not only a bird whisperer but an accomplished guitarist with "fleet-fingered fret-work" for a "New Orleans soul" band called Ross Griswold and the Second Line. "There are 1,800 rock-and-roll bands in New Jersey," he says of the reason to carve out a different niche.

"Who funds this?" asks an inquisitive visitor in front of the vulture enclosure.

"You do," Soucy replies. "I'll show you the donation box." Donations account for 93 percent of the facility's income. In 2016, $439,596 came from individual gifts and corporate support, $228,338 from foundation grants, $194,939 from sales and investments, and $23,975 from education programs and events. The Raptor Trust receives no state or federal funding.

"We have 20 foundations that we approach every year," Soucy explains. "Plus a lot of phil-anthropic people. We've had people who've mailed in a check [every year] for decades."

Plaques on the outdoor enclosures detail each bird: its size, habitat, range, and diet. Golden eagles are "very large, dark, long-winged birds and are North America's most formidable rap-tors," reads one marker.

The oldest resident is Uggla, a 38-year-old great horned owl. *Uggla* is Swedish for "owl." There's a barred owl named Sonny, after Len Soucy, whose nickname was Sonny. Several of the raptors go on the road on school visits—"a couple owls, a couple falcons, a couple hawks," Soucy says. "We feel that by keeping a few of them and using them for education purposes, we might be doing greater good."

Georgette, known for her "kack kack kack" calls at feeding time, was one of the "stars" of the education department according to the 2017 annual report. She was a female peregrine fal-con that fell from its nesting box atop the George Washington Bridge in 2002 and crash-landed on the pedestrian walkway below. The falcon was put in a cardboard box and brought to the Raptor Trust.

If you intend to drop off an injured bird, follow the instructions on the Raptor Trust website. Use a cardboard box to transport the bird; do not use a wire birdcage. Secure the bird by throw-ing a large towel or blanket over it. Gently but firmly lift the covered bird and lower it into the box. Keep the bird warm, dark, and quiet. Disturb as little as possible—do not give it water or food unless instructed. A common question—what do the birds admitted to the facility eat? The answer: tons of bugs. The Raptor Trust's annual insect budget is about $10,000 a year. In 2016, a total of 621,000 insects were used to feed the birds—524,000 mealworms, 76,000 crickets, 11,500 waxworms, 10,000 red worms, "and a delicious smattering of earthworms."

"People show up all the time with half a deer—'Wouldn't your vultures love this?' Yeah, but it might be poisoned," Soucy says. "We don't feed our birds any roadkill." He smiles. "Please don't bring the squirrels you find by the side of the road."

MUSCLE CARS FOREVER

THERE'S A CUTE LITTLE BUMPER car in the corner from Hershey Park, and I want it because bumper cars were my favorite childhood boardwalk ride, but then I spot a 1929 Ford Model rumble seat Roadster in the showroom—for only $17,000!—and I can see myself tooling around town in it. Then I come across a 1957 Chevy station wagon in the outside lot—with surfboards on the roof!—a dream set of wheels, especially for someone who lives Down the Shore . . .

There's way too much temptation at South Jersey Classics, on Route 40 in Pittsgrove. I had driven past the classic car business dozens of times in the past three years, never stopping. One day, I thought, this would make a good chapter, especially since I was doing a chapter on the demolition derby. One chapter on the joy of destroying cars, one chapter on the joy of owning and preserving them.

"It's a want, not a need," Ed Van Hee says of his customers. "They don't need it to get back and forth to work; it's to fulfill a dream."

Shawn Wark started South Jersey Classics in 2016 with nine cars, including a 1974 Corvette, a 1957 Buick Roadmaster, and a 22-foot Auburn Boat Tail Speedster replica. Wark opened his first car business, in Berlin, when he was 18 but saw a growing market in classic cars. He became friends with Van Hee, who had moved his detailing business across the street from Wark's first dealership, and in 2016, the two opened South Jersey Classics, building an addition and doubling the showroom space. There are about 70 cars here—see sjclassics.net for the full inventory—about 25 inside the showroom, the rest outside but well away from the road, since road salt is hell on chrome.

South Jersey Classics sells several hundred cars a year. Turnover is high. If you see something you like, don't wait forever to buy it. Where do they find the cars? Locals who know of the business. Estate sales. Internet ads. "Barn sales" are an increasingly popular source—"farmers who have classic cars they hide in their backyard barns," says Van Hee, whose ring tone is Wagner's "Ride of the Valkyries" and who talks fondly of his childhood Matchbox collection.

One of the cars on display is a 1931 Model A pickup; Wark bought it from a widow. "It was very emotional for her," Van Hee explains. "She held onto it for years before she was ready to let it go and she wanted to make sure it went to a good home."

The dealership has rabid overseas customers. Distance is not a barrier when you're crazy about classic cars.

"They like certain cars overseas," Van Hee notes. "Mustangs are very big, '60s early '70s Mustangs. DeLoreans. They went way down in value; now they're coming way up. Corvettes. Overseas, they like original cars." The representatives of two dealerships in France pay a visit to South Jersey Classics every six months to buy cars. The buyers make all the shipping arrangements. "They wire us the money," Van Hee says. "The most work we have to do is to get the car to the port [Newark]."

South Jersey Classics employs a full-time car scout—"He'll scout out areas, go in and talk to people," according to Van Hee. "We have ads online that say we buy cars. We end up meeting people at diners. [They say], 'Oh yeah Fred has a couple old cars he wants to sell,' and his barn is up the street next to the big white house, and you end up going out there, [meeting] people at 8, 9 o'clock at night, and making friends with them and buying their cars."

Even on vacation, he and Shawn will sometimes "sneak out" from their friends or families and check out cars or scour the local paper for ads.

Classic cars are a frequent sight on Main Streets and outside drive-in restaurants, but there are more organized classic car shows than you might think. The January 2019 issue of *NJ Cruise News*, which you can pick up at South Jersey Classics, listed shows in Montclair, Holmdel, Ocean City, Mahwah, Rahway, Wildwood, Morristown, Upper Township, Garwood, Atlantic City, Old Bridge, Piscataway, Wayne, Fanwood, Maplewood, Merchantville, Vincentown, West Deptford, Lakewood, Metuchen, and Califon. I might have missed one or two.

I liked the sound of the Modern Muscle Car Invasion, set for the Ocean City boardwalk and downtown in May. Five hundred cars are anticipated. That would be quite a sight. And so is South Jersey Classics' showroom, filled with grand, gorgeous cars. I ask Van Hee to pick out a half dozen cars in the showroom and tell their stories. He starts with a 1956 blue Corvette with a red interior. Just 3,467 'Vettes were made that year, the third-lowest production number in the history of the famed sports car.

"The paint is not the best quality, and we described it that way," Van Hee says. "If you look closely, you can see some minor popping underneath. It's an American icon; everyone loves the Corvette. The engine's been changed out with a later-model V8, so it's much more usable. It handles better." Asking price: $49,500.

We move on to a 1966 manual transmission Land Rover Santana.

"With locking differentials, high clearance points and short front/rear overhangs what obstacle would stand a chance against the Santana," reads the online description.

"Unique vehicles," Van Hee says. "They have their own following, people who absolutely love them."

Next car up is a baby blue 1966 Plymouth Belvidere, with a 472 stroked hemi. My favorite feature: the "altercation front suspension," which sounds like a great thing to have. The car was

The showroom at South Jersey Classics on Route 40, Pittsgrove

bought in Colorado. Wark sent an inspector out there to "confirm it was real, so we didn't have to fly out there," according to Van Hee. The new engine alone is worth about $45,000. Asking price for the car: $63,900.

"We strive for customer service and customer satisfaction," Van Hee notes. "We put the customer first. Most people in this industry put profit first. Others want to make $10,000 on a car; we make a thousand if we're lucky. But we move cars . . . and make people happy."

Then comes my favorite: a Model A original, restored in the 1980s, priced at $17,000.

"Fifteen years ago, we could have gotten $35,000," Van Hee says. The value on the Model As has dipped because their owners have passed away and their children don't share the same sentimental attraction to the car. The Model A is not built for the highway—"top speed is 45, and that's pushing it," according to Van Hee. It's great for maybe driving around the senior community or to the local Walmart and back.

"The old-timers, 80, 90, still enjoy these cars," he says.

Hey, I'm nowhere near 80, and I want that car!

The 1950 Mercury Custom Coupe is a gorgeous car, candy-apple red. "If you get a bunch of gear heads in a room together and they get to talking about the ultimate hot rod, inevitably there will be three constants on the list: the 1932 Ford Hi Boy Roadster, the 1932 Ford 3-window coupe and the 1950 Mercury coupe," reads the online summary.

"These are still sought after and can break six figures at auction," Van Hee says. "Paint—it's got some flaws in it. It's painted purple on one side and gray on the other side. Some people don't like that." The Merc is priced at $31,900.

The 1948 Lincoln just inside the door sure would look great in a remake of *The Untouchables*. A 350 V8 engine, manual windows, convertible top. It's a stunner. Price: $26,900.

One more car: a 1980 Camaro Z28 with 72,000 miles, red interior, original AM/FM stereo, and factory air.

"These are becoming more and more valuable," Van Hee says. "Five, six years ago, these weren't very valuable cars. The guys of this era have achieved some success, and they can buy one of these and put it away, and in another 5–10 years, they'll probably be worth $10,000 more than it is today.

"Muscle cars are always strong," he adds. "The Plymouths, the Challengers. That Belvidere, the Charger. They've all jumped up in value. The Mustangs, the Camaros, the Corvettes. They fluctuate a little, but they never die like the Model As have." He and Wark tell customers that buying a classic is "investing in fun. This is stronger than the stock market, stronger than your savings account. You can insure it and you can enjoy it. You can't enjoy your savings account, but you can enjoy driving in this."

Women make up 10–15 percent of their customers, who in general "range anywhere from their 20s to 70s and 80s," according to Van Hee. He just had a call from a 78-year-old man looking for a muscle car. "It's his last hurrah," Van Hee says, laughing.

He talks about an upcoming South Jersey Classics car show at the Showboat in Atlantic City. In previous years, South Jersey Classics took some of its cars to the annual classic car show at the Atlantic City Convention Center. The Showboat event is the dealership's first hosted show.

"We're going to bring 70–80 cars of our own to sell, . . . We may get 10 people, we may get 10,000 people [to attend]," Van Hee says. They've bought a nearby garage to store more cars, which means a bigger inventory and turnover.

At the moment, Wark is in Tennessee picking up a six-wheel 1992 Jeep with a hot tub trailer. Kenny Chesney was interested in buying it, according to Van Hee. The most expensive car they've sold was a Plymouth Superbird, known for its outrageous wings, for $170,000.

"At auction, some are doing a half million, six figures," Van Hee says of the car, made in 1969 and 1970 only. "They were ugly; people didn't like them," he says, laughing. "It wasn't known how many dealerships took the noses and wings off to sell the cars." They found the car in a barn in North Jersey; its owner had it for maybe 20 years.

"That was the Holy Grail, they're so sought after," Van Hee says. His favorite car on the lot is that 1956 'Vette. He's really enamored of it, so why doesn't he just buy it?

"Like Shawn said, we don't get married to the cars; we get married to our wives," Van Hee replies.

There's a cute little yellow 2000 adult go-cart in the office. Van Hee customized one, turning it into a high-end stroller for his daughter.

"When I take it on the boardwalk, people go berserk," he says, laughing.

Thirty, forty years from now, he sees himself and Wark still selling classic cars.

"It's not like work because it's fun every day," he says.

He's off to deal with several customers. I take one last look at that $17,000 Model A. I can just see myself tooling to the local Wawa in it. I might just have to make an offer.

DAVID BOWIE, *HIP HOP TUNNEL*, AND *AQUALAND*

ABOUT THE LAST PLACE YOU'D expect to find the director of a citywide mural arts program is a building where garbage trucks are parked, but Brooke Hansson's office is indeed located at the Jersey City public works headquarters. Her third-floor office is decorated with artwork—none of sanitation crews and trash bags as far as I could see—but she plays a key role in the cleaning up and beautification of what is soon to become the state's largest city.

"I'm a geek," she confesses. "I love being stationed in public works. We keep the city clean."

She's an artist, photographer, urban policy analyst, and documentary filmmaker (*What Happened to Jackson Avenue*) who runs the city's Mural Arts Program, formed in 2013 and funded by a Clean Communities grant. Its stated mission is to link "established and emerging local, national and international artists with property owners city-wide as part of an innovative beautification program that reduces graffiti, engages local residents and is transforming Jersey City into an outdoor art gallery."

About 140 murals commissioned by her office can be found around the city, from downtown to the Heights, the West Side, Greenville, and Journal Square. Artist stipends range from $800 to $3,000. Jersey City has become a street art hotbed. Besides the city's program, Green Villain, an arts organization, and Weehawken-based Savage Rabbit have commissioned artists to create murals.

"Murals are one of the only art forms that are truly for a community and they have helped create a greater dialogue between the community and art in general, generating more understanding of the importance of art in community," Inez Gradzki of Savage Rabbit told the *Jersey Journal*. Street art programs have popped everywhere from Philadelphia to Delhi and Mumbai (formerly Bombay), the latter two initiated by St+art India Foundation.

The Jersey City Mural Arts Program's most celebrated piece is one of late rocker David Bowie at 17th and Coles. International artist Eduardo Kobra created the kaleidoscopic 180-foot-high mural. Kobra, apparently a big Bowie fan, did not charge the city for his work, which took two weeks to execute.

"It's great to see that Jersey City has embraced street art through its mural program and I'm very happy to be a part of it," he told the *Jersey Journal*.

Hansson took me on a street art tour of Jersey City one crisp, clear morning; we stopped at 20 murals, including the Bowie artwork, a grand, shimmering sight in the morning sunlight.

It's even more spectacular lit up at night, a dazzling vision that can be seen by motorists on the turnpike extension leading to the Holland Tunnel.

"We call this SoHo—south of Hoboken," she says of the neighborhood. The other murals visited on our tour may have been smaller in scale but no less striking. There was Distort's *Peach Tree War*, a grandly eerie vision on an aging brick warehouse.

"The Peach War was a large-scale attack by the Susquehannock Nation and allied Native Americans on several Dutch settlements along the Hudson River," according to the artist's website (distoart.com). "The colonists believed the attack was motivated by the murder of a young Wappinger woman named Tachiniki, whom a Dutch settler killed for stealing a peach—an incident that had raised intercultural tensions shortly before the assault."

Another stop on our tour is an installment in Faith 47's ongoing project, *The Psychic Power of Animals*, at 316 Palisades Avenue. The series "brings the energy of nature back into the urban metropolis, softening the harsh city architecture with the gracefulness and spirit-like presence of the swans," according to the artist (faith47.com). "There's an inherent irony in re-creating nature on cement, so the series is a nostalgic reminder of what we've lost but also an attempt to reintegrate that into the present. We have become so distanced from nature, so these murals are an attempt to reconnect us with the natural world."

Long Lost Lenape Trail by Pawn & Emilio Florentine portrays an Indian woman with the stars and stripes emblazoned across her face; the mural, at Grand Street and Summit Avenue, is at the site of a former Lenape Indian trail. Beau Stanton's *Jersey City Crown* at 266 Newark Avenue (atop a Metro PCS store) is one of the mural arts program's grander pieces, a Zeus-like figure from whose head sprouts several iconic Jersey City buildings—the old City Hall, the Powerhouse, and New Jersey Central Terminal. Stanton spoke of street art's "wow" factor in an interview with juxtapoz.com.

"When you walk to work, and you come upon a mural or some sort of street intervention, it's the surprise factor," he said. "Just the fact that it can be experienced in your everyday life."

One of the more fun and playful works in the mural arts program is *Aqualand*, an underwater-themed piece that brightens a drab, block-long building at Grand Street and Johnston Avenue. Octopus, sharks, crabs, sea horses, starfish, and other marine life seem to swim right across the building. It's the creation of students in the mural arts program's six-week summer program, where students apprentice with local artists to create murals around the city.

The students work in small teams and are given step-by-step instruction in "public art techniques, including concept development, surface preparation, design enlargement, paint application and preservation techniques," according to the mission statement.

"I tell parents, I'm going to give your kid a can of paint and put them on a scissor lift," Hansson says. Many of the students had been "taggers"—graffiti artists—as Duda Penteado, an

The *Peach Tree War* by Distort is part of the Jersey City Mural Arts Program.

artist who worked with the mural arts program, noted in an interview with chickpeajc.com. They were "doing a few things they should not be doing," Penteado said. "They now have to go through the process and just learn the right thing to do with the tools."

"Coming up with the name was more for fun," Stardaysha, one of the students, told the website. "*Aqualand* is an underwater theme because Brooke thought the windows would look cool with fish swimming through it as if we're looking into an aquarium."

"It's quite amazing because every single person who participated has a different art style," Miriam, another student, added. "It's cool that you can see so many different things on just one wall."

We drive through the *Hip Hop Tunnel*, a 150-foot-long mural along New York Avenue that was once a graffiti-streaked mess. It's the work of artist William C. Richardson, who goes by the name Will Power. "We worked with Wally Wolf in the county, who had their electricians increase the lights inside the tunnel from 30 watts to 130 watts, transforming a dark, dingy, frequently littered and vandalized tunnel into a whole new world that is a delight to pass through," Richardson told hudsonreporter.com. About a dozen murals are added to the city's mural arts inventory every year; a handful are lost every year due to building demolition. The murals are painted by local artists, plus artists from 12 countries and six other cities.

Jersey City has been rated the nation's most ethnically diverse city, and the murals reflect the city's vibrant melting pot of cultures. Many of the murals can be found on the CANVS app, which offers detailed descriptions by the artists of the inspiration, materials, and execution of their work. The mural arts program's website is jcmap.org; on Instagram, it's @jcmap.

Buff Monster, a New York City artist who cites heavy metal, pop art, ice cream, Japanese culture, and graffiti among his major influences, painted *The Seven Heavenly Virtues* (581 Monmouth Street) as the flip side of his work *The Seven Deadly Sins* in Montreal. The Jersey City mural is part of the Mana Urban Arts Program (manacontemporary.com).

"This is by far the largest mural I've ever painted," Buff Monster says on CANVS. "It took 18 gallons of house paint just to prime it pink, and about 20 cans of spray paint to complete."

Shepard Fairey, described as "one of the most influential street artists of our time," has done murals in Jersey City for Mana Urban Arts and the city's mural arts program. One of the latter is *The Jersey Wave* at Grove Street Plaza, a large cresting wave with a backdrop of shiny office buildings. The mural symbolizes the "renaissance and cultural wave that Jersey City is riding while also acknowledging its waterfront location and the beauty and power of Mother Nature," according to CANVS.

The murals have turned Jersey City in a spectacular outdoor art museum, one easily accessible to all. There is another, much less glamorous, part of Hansson's job, though, and that is dealing with graffiti citywide.

"We have a graffiti problem, we really do," she says. She is always on the lookout for "tagged" buildings and objects. Those arrested for graffiti get sent to her; she assigns them to community service—painting traffic boxes around the city is a common task. When we spoke, she had just hired a "highly talented" artist in his 20s caught tagging. Initially, he painted traffic boxes and is now a contractor for the public works department. The mural arts program "is about arts and trends, but we have this grander ambition, to clean up a city in flux," Hansson explains.

It's time to head back to the public works headquarters and her office.

"This is nasty," she says, as we drive under a graffiti-streaked Conrail trestle. "I'm going to come back and clean it up."

I wouldn't be surprised if she was on it the next day.

I AM NOT EATING THE DIRT

A CANOE SLIPS THROUGH THE still waters. The rapturous silence takes your breath away. And John Volpa is telling me to never drink water near a beaver dam.

"The beavers constantly defecate in it," he says.

Oh, the things you learn when you're writing a book.

We are canoeing across Goshen Pond, minutes and a world away from Route 206 in Atsion. My biggest challenge is trying to paddle, take notes, and shoot video more or less at the same time. And trying not to lean too far to one side and capsize the boat.

Volpa is education director for Pinelands Adventures, responsible for its guided trips. Pinelands Adventures, headquartered in a cozy little cabin just off Route 206, is a part of the Pinelands Preservation Alliance, a private nonprofit dedicated to saving the Pinelands—that mysterious, magical, 1.1 million-acre swath of New Jersey. Sure, we've all heard about it, but how many of us have actually spent time there? (Driving through it on the way to somewhere else doesn't count.)

I'll be the first to admit my personal Pine Barrens experience hasn't amounted to a whole lot. I've written countless stories about the Pines and its woodsy wonder, but spending extensive time there, such as a canoe or camping trip?

Nope. At least not until 2008, when my then girlfriend and I camped outside in 25-degree weather in Wharton State Forest's Godfrey Bridge campground. Yes, outside, in a tent. Not surprisingly, we were the only ones there. Her sleeping bag, purchased two days before, worked swimmingly. Mine, last used during a backpacking trip to Alaska 30-plus years ago? Zipper wouldn't zip. Boy, was that a sleepless night (it zipped up fine when we got home, of course it did). So when the opportunity came to hop aboard a canoe with Volpa, I jumped at it, defecating beavers be damned.

"Two terms you've often heard—*Pinelands* and *Pine Barrens*," Volpa says before we board the canoe. "Pinelands refers to the Pinelands National Preserve, the only one of its kind in the United States, 1.1 million acres put together in 1979 . . . relegating development to the periphery and keeping the interior . . . as pristine as possible."

Pinelands Adventures' headquarters was once a canoe rental operation. The Pinelands Preservation Alliance bought the business to use "as an outreach center for our trips," says Rob Ferber, director of Pinelands Adventures. About 25,000 people have taken part in their programs since 2014—school and church groups, individuals. There are canoe trips, nature hikes,

Goshen Pond, just off Route 206, Pine Barrens

ghost town tours, and more; the two longest trips are Hike the Batona Trail and Rancocas River Guided Trip, both about eight hours.

"One year ago Pinelands Adventures was still just an idea," Ferber wrote on its website (pinelandsadventures.org) at the end of 2015. "It was a thoughtfully developed idea, and it was well on the way to becoming a reality, but it wasn't a done deal. By this time last year I had just been hired to run Pinelands Adventures. At that point, we still didn't own Adam's Canoe Livery and not much was certain, not even the name 'Pinelands Adventures.' We didn't have any staff, website or reservations system. Heck, we didn't even have a canoe!" They have dozens of canoes now and a year-round staff of 8, plus 8–10 seasonal employees.

Even if you don't immediately sign up for a trip, stop at the Pinelands Adventures office and pick up a copy of the Pinelands Preservation Alliance's excellent Pinelands Exploration

Map. The state publishes Pine Barrens & Beyond maps; you can view them online or order them at njwildlifetrails.org.

Volpa, a former environmental science teacher with Shamong Township Public Schools and the catalyst behind the creation of the Black Run Preserve in Evesham, proves an admirable guide and teacher on my Pine Barrens miniadventure. It started with a bumpy ride down an unmarked road past stands of sassafras and tupelo. We unload the canoe and slide it into the water. There is no one else around; nothing disturbs the silence.

Volpa talks about how chain pickerel, mud minnows, frogs, sunfish, and tadpoles can be indicators of low PH water, acidic water.

"In the swamp over there, you'll find the carnivorous plants. That's what gets the kids going—plants that eat bugs," he adds.

Talk inevitably turns to John McPhee and his 1968 book *The Pine Barrens*, which focused a national spotlight on the Pines.

"A lot of people give McPhee credit—all he did was draw attention to it and inspire Governor Brendan Byrne, the real hero of the story, to do something about it," Volpa says. "What drew McPhee here was the idea of the jetport in the 1960s [originally planned for North Jersey, in the Great Swamp, but that never came to fruition]. The people who fought it became the New Jersey Conservation Foundation. The people who fought it down in the Pine Barrens [were] conservationists, some of whom formed the Pinelands Preservation Alliance."

Howard Boyd was the best known, and certainly the most cantankerous, of those South Jersey conservationists. No one knew the Pine Barrens better; he was the Pine Baron. The author of *A Field Guide to the Pine Barrens of New Jersey* and three other books on the Pine Barrens, he initially worked for the Boy Scouts in Philadelphia. He made insect-collection trips in the Pine Barrens, eventually amassing a collection of about 50,000 insects (his favorite insect was the tiger beetle). For 20 years, he taught Pine Barrens ecology at the Conservation and Environmental Studies Center, later the Pinelands Institute for Natural and Environmental Studies, in Whitesbog. In 1989, he became involved with the Pinelands Preservation Alliance. I interviewed the Chatsworth resident in 2008. At one point, I asked if he would consider writing an autobiography.

"Who the hell am I?" he snapped. "It's too damn egotistical. Who wants to read a book on me?"

"But you're the Pine Barrens expert . . ."

"Call me what you want," he replies. "I don't care."

Unforgettable doesn't do Boyd justice. "One of the world's most unique natural areas" is how he described the Pine Barrens. He passed away in 2011.

"The name Pine Barrens," Volpa says as we glide across Goshen Pond, "was given by the early English settlers. The Dutch were the first to claim New Jersey; Henry Hudson sails up along the coast. But the Dutch focus mostly on North Jersey, the Hudson River, New Amsterdam, Bergen County. They're not interested in South Jersey at all, they're into making money, they immediately have horrible relations with the Lenni Lenape. It's the classic 'we're the white European civilized people and you're the savages,' and it doesn't go well from the very beginning. The English kicked the Dutch out in 1664 and came to divide New Jersey in half, East Jersey and West Jersey." The settlers called the area "the barrens." Volpa unfolds a copy of a map where the phrase "sandy barren deserts" is used to describe much of South Jersey.

"Because it [was] such a harsh environment—low nutrient, very acidic soil, [with] very hot, dry sandy soil in the summertime," he explains.

Ignorance about the Pine Barrens continues to this day. It makes up a quarter of New Jersey but largely does not register on the state consciousness. Ever see the Pine Barrens on a list of Top 20 Things to Do in New Jersey? Neither have I. There is no Pinelands Information Center, which could have alerted the crew of *The Sopranos* that the Jackson Whites, the characters Chris and Paulie discuss in the show's "Pines Barrens" episode, never lived there. That episode wasn't even filmed in the Pines but in New York state.

Maybe I should open a Pinelands information booth at one of the rest stops on the parkway or turnpike. Tell people about the 50-mile-long Batona Trail (stands for "Back to Nature"), marked with pink blazes, winding past long-gone towns such as Martha and Lower Forge. About Route 542, from New Gretna to Hammonton, maybe my favorite Jersey road (partly because I often seem to be the only person on it). About places such as the Lower Bank Tavern and the Oyster Creek Inn and Lucille's Café in Warren Grove. I won't bring up the middle-of-the-freezing-night, sleeping-bag-wouldn't-zip-up fiasco unless prompted. Volpa, or anyone at Pinelands Adventures for that matter, would be better equipped to handle the Pine Barrens PR job anyway.

When he talks to schoolkids about good and bad soil for farming, Volpa lets the brave ones taste the soil.

Wait, taste dirt?

"I grew up on a farm," he says, laughing. "My grandfather used to put dirt in his mouth, tell you if it was sweet or sour."

One thing that visitors here are happy to learn—poison ivy is practically nonexistent.

"The bane of my childhood," I say, then proceed to tell Volpa about the severe case of poison ivy I had 20 years ago that managed to freak out the nurses at the Maine hospital I visited (they had never seen it so bad).

The number one reason why the Pinelands National Preserve exists? The 17 million gallons of water in the ground.

"I know the water's pure—can you actually drink it?" I ask.

"Excellent question," Volpa says. "Biologists have classified every aquatic insect into one of three categories based on [how] well they can tolerate pollution. Class 1 bugs can't tolerate any pollution whatsoever. Class 2 bugs, *menz a menz*, a little bit. Class 3 is nasty—no oxygen [in the] water. Mosquito larva, maggots, nasty stuff. So if you find bugs from mostly category 1 and category 2, they are telling you the water's clean enough to drink. Throughout the world, monthly biologists are going out to reservoirs and rivers checking to make sure the bugs are saying this is clean enough to be used as a water source." It's the kind of inside information you get on Pinelands Adventures trips.

It's also time to head back to the little cabin Pinelands Adventures calls home; Volpa has a program to lead in the afternoon.

On the way home, I'm already thinking of my next, more extended, Pine Barrens adventure, one that will hopefully not include poison ivy, stuck zippers, or dirt eating.

LIVES REBUILT, HOPES RESTORED

THE WORLD'S LARGEST SALAD—OR AT least the largest salad in New Jersey this particular day, enough to feed 150—fills an industrial-sized pot on the stainless-steel table. The salad, with Romaine and iceberg lettuce, cherry and regular tomatoes, peas, onions, and cucumbers, is topped with creole mustard dressing, black pepper, oregano, and parsley. To one side of the table is dessert: Krispy Kreme donuts, minimuffins someone bought at Kings, coconut custard pies donated by the Hudson School in Hoboken by way of BJs.

The "first course" tonight is a batch of peanut butter and jelly sandwiches made by members of a church in Caldwell.

"Every night is an episode of *Chopped*," says John, the kitchen cook/manager. "Every night I walk in, I don't know what I'm getting into."

Dinner is about to be served at the Hoboken Shelter. Three meals a day, every day of the year, are served at the shelter, which opened in 1982. Some might say, homeless people in Hoboken? In the state's toniest town?

Yes, not only in Hoboken but in Hudson County in general. The shelter feeds 500-plus people every day. Since 1982, it has served three million meals and housed a half million "guests." In 2005, the shelter served 55,000 meals. In 2019, it served about 200,000 meals. The numbers and need are not about to lessen.

"Home-cooked meals," says Jaclyn Cherubini, "are the best way to show someone's loved." She is the shelter's executive director. Mark Singleton, president of the shelter's board of directors, calls Cherubini, a Douglass College graduate and former assistant director at Pathways to Housing in NYC, "our fearless leader who is like a whirling dervish on too much espresso."

The shelter is owned and operated by Communities of Faith for Housing Inc., a non-profit housing corporation made up of ministers and laity from houses of worship as well as several Hoboken community leaders. It is housed on the ground floor of St. John's Lutheran Church, at the corner of Bloomfield and Third streets. The dining room and men's housing are on the ground floor; the women sleep upstairs.

"This is where the women sleep at night," says Cherubini inside the church's nave, reached by steep, winding stairs. Beds are kept in a side room. "The tables get folded up, the beds get rolled out," she says.

Volunteers making an enormous salad inside the kitchen at the Hoboken Shelter

Evening workshops are held upstairs. There is a Monday art class and a Wednesday creative writing class; other workshops are held downstairs.

"We do a lot with a little," Cherubini says. About 10,000 volunteers work here over the course of a year. The number doesn't include people who walk in off the street with donated food.

A man in his 30s accompanied by his young daughter walks into the kitchen and drops off two turkeys.

"That will help us feed 50 people," Cherubini tells him.

The shelter is in constant need of food and supplies. The top food needs: milk, coffee, sugar, cereal, juice, frozen meat. The top supply needs: paper/plastic plates, hot/cold cups, napkins, plastic utensils, hand sanitizer. Toiletries: soap, shampoo, toothbrushes, toothpaste, deodorant.

John, the kitchen manager (first names are used for several people in this chapter due to privacy reasons), was a volunteer "on and off for nine years," he says.

"He has a talent for making something out of nothing," Cherubini says. "He should be on *Chopped*."

Dara, a guest, has been coming to the shelter for two months, since mid-September. "I'm hoping to be in my apartment in December," she says. "I'm hoping and praying."

There's Johnny, with tiny crucifixes decaled on his glasses, beneficiary of the shelter's Supportive Housing Program; and Eli, a volunteer here for seven years. Has he ever missed a day?

"Never," he says proudly.

James Shipman has been a volunteer for 21 years. What does he do?

"Anything and everything is the short version," he says, laughing. "Basically, we help people deal with any crisis in their [lives]. A lot of mental health stuff, [drug/alcohol] abuse stuff. It can be anything."

On the shelter's website, Singleton detailed the shelter's sometimes perilous journey over the years: "I count as a moment of Divine intervention that moment when the initial communities of Faith got together and said, 'We have to do something [about the growing problem of homelessness and hunger in Hoboken]' or when the Congregation of St. John's said, 'You can use our church hall.' And here we are 30 years later . . . in this quiet place of refuge . . . and trust . . . and peace. God is good."

There have been close calls when the shelter's future was imperiled.

"More than once, we were on the verge of losing this place," Singleton said. "From lawsuits to the city challenging our right to shelter, to unpaid water liens, and most recently, to falling roof beams."

The shelter's accomplishments? "Meals in the millions, beds in the hundreds of thousands, and no way to count the number of families reunited, lives rebuilt, addictions battled, dreams rekindled, hopes restored," Singleton added. He and his friend Eddie started cooking chicken legs, yellow rice, gravy, and salad at the shelter in 1984 and became known as the Chicken People.

"Today, I am a 50-year-old man who has never missed a second Wednesday of the month since," Singleton said.

Fifty percent of the shelter's guests were born and raised in Hoboken, 45 percent in other parts of Hudson County, according to Cherubini.

"It's a testament to the community that we have a shelter next to three-million-dollar houses," she says.

Finding housing is as important as fighting hunger. In 2016, the shelter helped 148 men and women move from the street to the shelter to their own homes; in 2018, the number was 184. The Supportive Housing Program, funded by the federal Department of Housing and Urban Development (HUD), houses 36 men and women in their own apartments.

The shelter runs on a schedule. At 6 a.m., lights go on, and it's time to get up. Breakfast is from 9–11 a.m. Noon to 2 p.m., shower time. "Anyone who needs a hot shower can get one," Cherubini says. At 1:30, a hot lunch is served. "We serve a lot of chicken," she says, smiling. From 3–5 p.m., there's a movie in the main room downstairs. This particular day, it's *The Patriot*.

"It's such a human thing to watch a movie when you're on the street," according to Cherubini. "It's a great time to rest and relax and recover." At 5:30 p.m., snacks are put out, and at 7:15, dinner is served. At 10 p.m., it's lights out.

Volunteers from St. Ann's Church in Hoboken are hosting tonight's dinner—baked ziti and meatballs and that salad for 150. Tiffany Kane, a schoolteacher in Jersey City who is in charge of the kitchen crew tonight, volunteers two Tuesdays a month.

Restaurants and supermarkets regularly donate food—La Isla drops off 80–100 chicken legs each week. Trader Joe's unloads a truckload of food every Saturday, and more food comes from farmers markets in Hoboken and Jersey City.

"Choco-Pan gives us bread every morning, Dunkin' Donuts drops off donuts," Cherubini says. "Realtors give us leftovers from their open houses."

The guests' favorite meal: meatloaf. Favorite drink: coffee. Chili's on the menu every other Tuesday, meatloaf the fourth Wednesday of each month. Some guests might avail themselves of the meals and other services for several days, some for weeks or months. It's not just the homeless but the working poor and people going through difficult times.

"I've had firefighters, policemen, construction workers, nurses, social workers, teachers, professionals, you name it," Cherubini says.

About one-third of the shelter's funding comes from what Cherubini calls "generous individuals in the faith-based community." Another third comes from government grants—"and that's shrinking"—the remainder from fund-raisers, including an annual winter auction that raises about $30,000.

"I can't close our doors; people need to eat," Cherubini says.

At 7:02 p.m., John, the kitchen manager, tells his crew, "So we're two or three minutes away from bringing everything over."

At 7:10, there's a quick tutorial. "Before we go out, I'm going to show you portion sizes."

In the dining room, guests wait quietly and patiently. Some play cards, others peer at smartphones. Guests overall are divided: one-third white, one-third African American, and one-third Latino, according to Cherubini.

"These are not Hollywood homeless," she points out. "We're not what we see on TV, that little old lady or that crackhead guy. We're helping people get housing, we're trying to get them work."

One word she hates using: *homeless*. "I say 'the homeless' a gazillion times a year. It's the word I hate the most. Nobody calls you by what you don't have."

This particular night, the shelter is celebrating everyone's birthday. Doesn't matter whether it's your birthday or not. Small gifts are handed out, there is cake, and slips of paper offer appropriate wisdom from Dr. Seuss: "Today you are you! That is truer than true. There is no one alive who is you-er than you! Shout loud, I am lucky to be what I am! Thank goodness I'm not just a clam or a dusty old jar of sour gooseberry jam. I am what I am! That's a great thing to be!"

Cherubini asks Tiffany Kane to blow out the candles. The shelter's executive director looks out at the men and women in the dining room. "Everyone, make a wish," she says. "My wish is that everyone gets housing. Let's all try to make that wish come true."

THE STATE'S COOLEST SPOT

I AM SITTING IN MY Jeep near the corner of Fourth and High in Elizabeth with a cup of lemon ice and one thought: I want to pour the sweet, ice-cold treat over my head.

It's that hot out.

OK, I actually didn't do that, instead quickly licking the ice—it was melting fast—the blinding heat temporarily forgotten.

On one of those July afternoons where the heat and humidity suck the air and life out of you, there's no better place to be than DiCosmo's Italian Ice in the Peterstown section of Elizabeth. Don't go expecting some shiny, spotless stand with a big menu board displaying dozens of flavors. DiCosmo's is a little green shack with a green, white, and red awning—the colors of the Italian flag. There are no more than four flavors at any one time, and when they run out of one flavor, well, you just have to try something else.

This is the state's best Italian ice; I dare you to find one better. That nationwide chain ice? Please.

"Lemon is the most popular flavor, coconut a close second, then pineapple," John DiCosmo says.

More than 100 years after opening as a grocery store, DiCosmo's Italian Ice not only survives but thrives. There's no website. There's not even a sign outside DiCosmo's, just lettering on one of the windows. The faithful know where the green shack is: Fourth and High.

Caterina and Giovanni DiCosmo, John's grandparents, opened their grocery store, then on John Street, in 1915.

"Of all Peterstown, that was the most Italian street," John says. He and his wife, Nancy, are sitting at the dining room table in their house. A group photo of their six kids when young—all wide-eyed and beaming—is on the wall. On the table is a box of *sfogliatelle* from Calandra's in Newark, still warm from John's dawn trip there. "They were hot in the box; I almost [ate them]," he confesses. Around 1920, Caterina and Giovanni bought the house where John and Nancy live today. Next door is the Italian ice stand, and in the summer, John and Nancy can often be found sitting on their lawn chairs out front. You don't have to go far to find the owners.

Caterina and Giovanni sold cheese, canned goods, and soda at the beginning. But not ice, not just yet. Caterina would make ice for friends, but the couple didn't start selling it until

The tiny DiCosmo's Italian Ice stand in Elizabeth

1918 when Giovanni built the shack. They sold ice (lemon only), candy, cigars, grocery items. The ice would be frozen inside barrels, the same way it's made today.

There were at least five Italian ice stands in Elizabeth in the early 1900s; DiCosmo's is the only one still around. Agnes DiCosmo, John's mother, "came into the picture" in 1939, introducing pineapple and orange ice—later, berries and peach.

"His grandmother swore nobody would ever eat [those flavors]," Nancy said, laughing. "But they did." John's grandmother and grandfather started the store, but Agnes was known as "the lemon ice lady of Peterstown."

Helping out was Lucy Rainone, known as "Lucy Lemons," a local character. "She was sometimes nasty to people, but to our children, she was great," Nancy says.

Bobby Minetta would bring the lemons, and George the iceman would deliver blocks of ice, which would be cut up and placed between the wooden barrels and the stainless-steel churning machine. Agnes kept the ice in 10 unplugged refrigerators out back. Didn't the ice melt?

"Slowly," Nancy replies.

So how is ice made? "We put stainless steel canisters in our old wooden barrels, with ice and rock salt in between the two," John told the *New York Times* in 1996. "Then I pour a mixture of fruit juice, sugar and water into the canisters. Metal dashers are lowered into the liquid, and they mix it back and forth for about 40 minutes. No ice is added; it freezes slowly because it's packed in ice."

In 1996, he says, three new flavors were introduced: white grape, four berry (strawberry, blackberry, raspberry, blueberry), and mixed fruit with watermelon. In the mid-'80s, John and Nancy switched to Italian ice only—no more candy and groceries—and started making it inside the little green shack.

Most famous customer ever? That would probably be Frank Sinatra.

"My mother-in-law said he came here, didn't get out of his car," Nancy says.

The city's Peterstown section is known as The Burg. You won't go hungry around here. Spirito's, one of the state's great old-school restaurants, is within walking distance of DiCosmo's, and so are hot dog landmarks Tommy's Italian Sausage & Hot Dogs and Jerry's Famous Frankfurters. The shack opens at noon, although John's day starts around seven with shopping, peeling fruit, and other duties. DiCosmo's always opens by Memorial Day, sometimes in April if the weather's good. They close for the season at the end of September or early October. When closing day approaches, some diehards will pick up 10, 20 quarts to store them in the freezer for their winter stash. The operation seems low-rent, but DiCosmo's is surprisingly social media–savvy. Nancy gives daily flavor updates on Facebook like this one:

> Good Morning All, what a beautiful Sunday morning it is. Today's starters will be Orange, Coconut & Chocolate. We do not have a date set yet to close, but we will keep everyone posted as soon as we decide or should we say, Mother Nature decides. 12:00–7:00 or until sold out, weather permitting. See you later, stock up now!!!

Nancy also gives weather reports, especially on rainy days (when the stand is closed) and hot days.

> Good Morning Everyone, it's gonna be a scorcher today & tomorrow, so why not cool off with us!!! Today's starters will be Orange/Pineapple, Coconut, Lemon & Cherry. 12:00–8:00 or until sold out, always weather permitting.

Customers, especially those from out of state, chime in on how much they miss their ice. Here's one example:

> Coming in from Texas on Wednesday. Heading straight to you. Sure hope you are open and have lemon. It has been two years since my last fix.

Fix, indeed. This ice is addictive. I'm glad I don't live anywhere near Elizabeth; I'd be at DiCosmo's four, five times a week in the summertime. Maybe four, five times a day. There are four flavors each day, but when each flavor runs out, that's it, come back tomorrow or whenever it's next available. There's a handy DiCosmo's app where you can see what flavors are available each day. How many businesses tell a celebrity chef to get lost? This one did. Guy Fieri wanted to do a segment on DiCosmo's Rockaway Beach store, but Nancy and John turned him down. The crew wanted to film in the kitchen, but the couple said no—"you can't go into the kitchen." Only family allowed there.

There's one more rule at DiCosmo's: only John and Nancy make the ice. Not their children, not the kids they hire for the summer, not nobody. Their son, John, ran the Rockaway Beach store; he added such funky flavors (for Italian ice anyway) as green tea and avocado.

"I told John, your grandmother is turning over in her grave," Nancy said. The Rockaway store was destroyed during Hurricane Sandy, and their daughter Eileen ran a Surf City, NJ, DiCosmo's for three years. Eileen says her son and daughter may "apprentice" at the little green shack this coming summer.

Lemon ice is almost always on hand, but much depends on availability, price, and quality of fruit.

"We had watermelon this year because we had good watermelon," Nancy explains. The summer before, the watermelon had "no flavor. It was wet, heavy," she adds. Citrus prices exploded the summer of 2018, and that had an effect on the stand's benchmark flavor.

"It was $100 a box," John relates. "We didn't make lemon ice for a couple weeks." Customers were not happy. No lemon? What kind of ice stand is this? Most of the fruit comes from South Jersey farmers (lemons and oranges from Restaurant Depot).

Most dramatic day in DiCosmo's history? About eight years ago, when a teenage driver crashed into the store—fortunately at night, unfortunately, the day before they were set to open for the summer. The accident caused $60,000 worth of damage and delayed the stand's opening for six weeks.

John's grandparents are from Volata, just north of Naples, and his wife is Irish.

"We've been to Ireland twice to visit someone's relatives," he says, smiling. They've never been to Italy, which they hope to correct soon. Both are in their 60s. "I can see us hanging in for a few more years," Nancy says. Then, hopefully, one of their kids will take over.

Their secret all these years?

"Just doing one thing," John says succinctly.

"Being family-oriented," Nancy adds. "I like to think the customers are as happy with our product as my family is. It warms my heart."

My 25 Favorite Ice Cream Shops/Stands

Bent Spoon, Princeton. Named after an object in *The Matrix*, the Bent Spoon was opened in 2004 by Gabrielle Carbone and Matt Errico, who met at the College of New Jersey. They're still at it, overseeing a tiny, perpetually packed shop on Palmer Square. They're big on using locally sourced ingredients, and the ice cream is both terrific in quality and eclectic in range. Dad's Hat Rye Whiskey sea salt caramel, anyone? My favorites: the blood orange and blue lemon. And I still remember the chocolate habanero ice cream that I had there 10 years ago.

Charlie's Homemade Ice Cream, Seaside Park. I'm going to catch serious grief for not including legendary Hoffman's in Point Pleasant Beach on this list, but I think Charlie's is better. Charlie's has been open 35 years, yet I keep running across people who've never heard of it. I can't live without chocolate ice cream, and they do chocolate about as well as anyone—regular chocolate, chocolate fudge brownie, and my favorite, the Jamaican almond fudge.

Cliff's Homemade Ice Cream, Ledgewood. Best ice cream flavor in New Jersey? The double dark chocolate fudge crunch at Cliff's. I'm getting dizzy just thinking about it. The Route 46 stand was opened in 1975 by Cliff Freund, an ice-cream salesman and teacher at Roxbury High School. There are 60-plus flavors of hard ice cream, so it's OK if it takes a while to decide.

Cookman Creamery, Asbury Park. It's not easy being the coolest kid on the block in New Jersey's hippest town, but Cookman Creamery pulls it off with a great vibe and an excellent product. The owners are the father-son duo of Jimmy and Mike Johnson, who kept most of the recipes from the previous owners, a mother-daughter duo. Collaborations with local restaurants are often in play; they did one with Speakeatery that included salted caramel ice cream with cinnamon espresso from the local sandwich shop and hot fudge swirls. Oh, and I dare you to taste any difference between their regular and vegan ice cream.

Cow's Brow, Fredon. Jake Hunt, the ice cream maker at Windy Brow Farms, is the mad scientist of the Jersey ice cream world. He unleashed a Taylor ham ice cream in 2018 (it was quite good, more like a rich maple ice cream with pork roll bits), and if that wasn't enough, he also dropped a tomato pie flavor several months later. The base was made with oregano, black pepper, red pepper flakes, cumin, and Italian seasoning, with SunGold tomato jam, ricotta cream, and basil oil added later. Hunt also made cranberry creamsicle, sweet corn and honey, and buttermilk and blueberries for what he called his Only in Jersey collection. Regular flavors include milk chocolate, honey lavender, coconut blueberry lime, cold brew coffee, and grapefruit rosemary sorbet.

Cream Valley Custard, Woodstown. It may be ice cream heresy, but the soft serve at Cream Valley Custard—swirly, soft, and über-creamy—is every bit as good, if not better, than fabled Kohr's Down the Shore. The stand opened in 1973 and is owned by Nancy Wilson, who worked here when she was in high school.

Das' Creamery, Budd Lake. Das' Creamery pushes the ice cream envelope like few others, with whimsically titled flavors that belie the seriousness that goes into making each one. Owner Komal Das and her dad, Panka ("I'm just the assistant," he says), make the ice cream. The most popular flavor at the bright, cheery shop is Colombian cookie and cream. Indulge your wild side with some cinnamon almond tipsy raisin (made with rum-soaked raisins), basil Junior Mint, or the sweet cream blueberry. My favorites: chocolate (no surprise there), mango, village fig.

Fajji's Homemade Ice Cream, Perth Amboy. There's no Fajji at Fajji's Homemade Ice Cream—he was an employee of the former owners—but current owner Tom Griffin doesn't mind if you call him Fajji. "They buy my ice cream, they can call me anything they want," he says. The staff wears tie-dyed T-shirts, and many of the flavors are Caribbean-accented, including coconut (Griffin cracks the coconuts himself), pineapple, and passion fruit. My favorites: Thin Mint cookie and deep chocolate.

Gelotti, Paterson. It started as Boonstra Dairy; at one time, the dairy leased space in back from a funeral home. Today, Gelotti is easy to find; it's next to a cemetery. There are 40 kinds of ice cream and about 20 kinds of gelato, including *bacio* (Italian hazelnut); *amarena* (bourbon vanilla flavored with sour cherries), melon, peach, strawberry, and coconut.

Guernsey Crest Ice Cream Co., Paterson. If you drive right by Guernsey Crest the first time, it's understandable. Practically hidden along 19th Avenue, and sharing the neighborhood with Bergen Lift Truck, United Motor Collision, and Swift Lube, the neighborhood ice cream shop is not much for appearances inside or out, but it's a longtime locals-only hangout. There's no website and a barely there Facebook page. Find it—that's half the challenge—and enjoy.

Halo Pub, Princeton. It's not a bar but an ice cream shop—and one often overlooked in a town with Bent Spoon and Thomas Sweet. Their chocolate rocks, and don't forget to try their sorbet.

Ice Cream by Mike, Ridgewood. In 2018, Mike Elias moved from cramped quarters in Hackensack to a bigger, brighter spot in Ridgewood. He uses high-end ingredients and is always releasing creative if not crazy flavors. You're not going to find 40–50 flavors here; more like 10. Try the French vanilla or lemon ice cream; you'll thank me later. I'll surely take heat for not picking local legends Bischoff's or Conrad's or Van Dyk's, but I've been to all three, and Ice Cream by Mike is better.

Latteria, Swedesboro. This is the state's most colorful ice cream shop, with tables and walls painted in swirly kaleidoscopic colors—think Cezanne and van Gogh meet Peter Max over ice cream. "Our cream is from farms that take care of the animals and land," says a sign. My favorites: the dark chocolate and toasted coconut.

Luigi's Ice Cream, Jersey City. "Pete, keep an eye out for the test tube ice cream," Luigi Beltran warned me at the beginning of our NJ's Best Ice Cream Showdown for nj.com. "Most of these ice cream shops operate their kitchen like a high school chemistry lab. Add a little #004 yellow food coloring and mix it with 5 CCs of mango flavor extract and voilà—mango ice cream! Unless you're peeling dozens of mangos and painstakingly separating the mango fruit from the seed, then it ain't mango ice cream!"

Well, OK! Beltran's truck is a familiar sight in Jersey City; he wowed the ice cream world when he opened the state's first "ice cream speakeasy" inside Ani Ramen in Jersey City, with boozy—alcoholic—flavors. My favorite: Hennessy and pineapple. Sweet, sensuous, and borderline sinful.

Mackey's Orchard, White. Some of New Jersey's best ice cream is made at its farms (see also the entry for Cow's Brow). At Mackey's, the hard ice cream comes from an outside vendor; you'll want to try the homemade soft serve, made with fruits in season—strawberry, blueberry, peach, and black raspberry. The latter is pretty close to incredible.

Maple Shade Custard Stand, Maple Shade. My second-favorite soft serve in the state next to Serene Custard (see separate entry), and yes, both are better than legendary Kohr's or Kohr Bros (and I love both of those!). The red-and-white-trimmed Maple Shade Custard Stand, which dates back to the '50s, is a scoop of vanishing Americana with its walk-up counter and "Drive In" sign atop the roof. It's first-rate soft serve: smooth and colossally creamy.

Milk Sugar Love, Jersey City. Emma Taylor started with an ice cream cart at local farmers' markets; she now owns two stores in Jersey City, one across from Hamilton Park, the other in the Heights. There are about a dozen or so flavors to choose from. Her chocolate peppermint ice cream was the best thing I ate in all of 2013. I still remember driving home in a snowstorm with a container and scooping out spoonfuls whenever I stopped.

Nasto's Ice Cream Co., Newark. One of the Ironbound's great food legends, Nasto's opened in 1939 in a former brewery. Secret to its long life? "Put the good stuff in and get good stuff out," Frank Nasto III once told me. The blue-awninged store supplies ice cream to 750 or so restaurants around New Jersey. And don't forget about the *tartuffo*, spumoni, tortoni, and fresh fruit sorbets in the display case.

Owowcow Creamery, Lambertville. In summer 2016, I visited 41 ice cream shops around New Jersey in our NJ's Best Ice Cream Showdown (tough job, but someone had to do it). Owowcow Creamery emerged as the winner. Their slogan is "Passionately made, warmly shared," and the ice cream dazzles with its combination of classic and nontraditional flavors. There are Tahitian, Madagascar, and Indonesian flavors of vanilla ice cream, plus such head-spinners as lime cilantro, blueberry lemon, and cinnamon bourbon. The mint chocolate chip may be the best I've had anywhere.

Royale Crown Homemade Ice Cream and Grille, Hammonton. Hammonton is the blueberry capital of the world, so it comes as no surprise that Royale Crown makes blueberry ice cream—make that unbelievably good blueberry ice cream. The diner-shiny ice cream stand opened in 1953 on the White Horse Pike. Waitresses back then wore white majorette boots, short skirts, and gold crowns. There are about 40 kinds of hard ice cream and 8 flavors of soft ice cream. Another must-try: the black raspberry soft serve.

Serene Custard, Vineland. Best soft serve in New Jersey? This stand, on the other side of the railroad tracks in the state's largest city by size, opened in 1959; current owner Ed Rone took over in 1984. His wife, Linda, makes the ice cream, although Ed did build the miniature golf course out back. He uses an expensive mix, and it shows. The result is rich and creamy and colder than any soft serve I've tried.

Springer's Homemade Ice Cream, Stone Harbor. Open since Prohibition, Springer's was Taylor Swift's favorite ice cream hangout when she summered here. There are 50-plus flavors on the board, so if you don't find something you like, there is probably something wrong with you. Recommended: the Dark Nite (black raspberry chocolate chip) or Prohibition Tradition (Kahlua ice cream with fudge swirl). Don't be discouraged by the ever-present line; it moves pretty quick.

Summer Ville Homemade Ice Cream, Somerville. Computer-tech-turned-ice-cream-maker Elio DeFranco is the owner of Summer Ville Homemade Ice Cream. Furnishings? Some came from Craigslist, including a fearsome-looking hammerhead shark replica. At an estate sale, he found himself in a bidding war with an elderly woman over a wooden whale, a war he was determined not to lose. The whale hangs in the middle of the store, where about 40 flavors are written on bright, colorful placards on the wall. The most popular flavor here is Somerville Mud (chocolate chip cookies, M&Ms, Reese's Pieces, Oreos); kids have been known to burst into tears when they discover the shop's out of it. No Mud? Try the key lime, my favorite.

Torico Ice Cream, Jersey City. This casually stylish ice cream parlor does traditional and offbeat flavors; the latter include *ube* (purple yam), pound cake, and cherry pistachio. My favorites: black sesame, pineapple coconut, ginger. The business traces its roots to 1968, when Peter and Pura Berrios, from Puerto Rico, started making slushes and sorbets in a former deli. The name is a contraction of *todo rico*—"everything is delicious." Denise Berrios and her son, Steven, now make the ice cream; Christine Berrios, Denise's sister, helps run the business.

UMMM Ice Cream Parlor, Burlington City. This may be the most beautifully retro ice cream shop in the state, with wooden booths and chairs. It was once a detective agency, hearing aid store, and maybe a bookie joint. And it's a serious seller of Boost! (see separate chapter). Owner Matt Garwood loves to experiment with flavors; oddball ones have included pickle and candied bacon. My favorite: the chocolate-covered espresso bean and the Rosanna Banana Dana, a tribute to Gilda Radner's character on *Saturday Night Live*.

BABY, YOU CAN CRASH MY CAR

THE BATTERED CARS, IN GLORIOUSLY garish shades of purple, green, red, and orange, with sponsor and driver names (Beast Mode, Cave Man Racing, the Punisher) painted on hoods and side panels, chug and wheeze their way to a dirt track at New Egypt Speedway. There is a smattering of fans in the stands on this rainy day, but no matter.

The eight drivers, seven men and one woman, would be here in rain, snow, sleet, or hail—crashing their cars into each other; inflicting metal-crunching carnage, hoods cringing and trunks collapsing; trash talking when they're not recoiling from another teeth-chattering hit.

Demolition derby lives. You might have thought it went the way of 8-track tapes and stick shifts, but "demo" is a staple at county and state fairs, special events, and racetracks across the country. There are certainly not as many derbies as in the boom times of the 1960s and 1970s, but scores are held every year, from 8- or 10-driver mashups to 50-plus car events. The self-described World's Largest Demolition Derby, with about 100 cars participating, is held annually at the Erie County Fairgrounds in Hamburg, NY (the largest-ever demolition derby featured 123 cars at Mount Maunganui, New Zealand, in 2002). The USA Demolition Derby Co., founded 44 years ago, hosted 34 demos in Michigan in 2019. The International Demolition Derby held 19 events in Indiana, Illinois, Wisconsin, Michigan, and West Virginia. There's the Woodbooger Demolition Derby in Taunton, MA, and the Goshen Stampede Derby in Goshen, CT—not to be confused with the Stampede Demolition Derby in Greeley, CO. There's even a School Bus Demolition Derby at Riverhead Raceway on Long Island.

"Kids get a kick out of seeing school buses they ride every day get destroyed," raceway co-owner Tom Gatz told *Newsday*. "They find it neat to watch them get smashed up."

The New Jersey State Fair / Sussex County Farm & Horse Show had a derby in 2019, and so did the Warren County Farmers' Fair & Balloon Festival, the Cumberland County Fair, Wall Stadium, and New Egypt Speedway.

The eight contestants at the New Egypt demo in October were a colorful, chatty crew, and they all seemed to be named Lane. No, really. There was Norman Lane Sr., the patriarch of a demo family that includes Norman, his son; his nephew, Robert Lane; Wesley Lane, Robert Lane's cousin; and Norman Lane Sr.'s "almost daughter-in-law," Amy LaBella, his son's girlfriend. Oh, and Norman Lane Sr.'s father was also a Norman. His grandson's name? Take one guess.

What does a car look like after a demolition derby? Like this.

"I don't run these little cars," Norman Lane Sr. said dismissively. "Hurts too much. I'm not driving today. I let the kids do the little cars. The next day you can't move, you're all stiff."

Tom DeSantis ("Everybody calls me Dick Santis because of my personality. I'm known to be an asshole") was driving a 1998 Camry. It's his second season as a demo driver. "I got dared" by a friend to do it, he says. "I got suckered into it." He's an electronics mechanic for the Port Authority of New York / New Jersey. His responsibility: repairing subway turnstiles.

DeSantis is driving a 1998 Camry with what looks like black and red teeth painted on the doors. He says it's on borrowed time; it breaks down too often.

"I can't get a decent ride out of it," he moans. "I'm giving it one last chance. This car dies today, I'm cutting it up [for parts]." He owns 10 junkers at the moment, all destined for the derby. You can always find cars on Facebook.

"I'm missing my brother's baby shower," DeSantis confesses. "I showed up at his house with the car on the trailer, dropped off his gift." His demo buddy, Billy Strathern, in the Beast Mode car, stands nearby. The two met when Tom bought a car off Billy's dad. Billy's father, grandfather, and two aunts all did demo at the Warren County fairgrounds. Billy drove his first car when he was 16; he's now 29. He says there are youth demo leagues in Pennsylvania for 10- to 12-year-olds.

"Those little kids hit just as hard," he points out. Robert Lane, usually a driver but representing a sponsor today, has participated in a dozen demos.

"I've never lost," he says matter-of-factly. His dad is Ron Lane Sr., a former demolition derby world champion. One car is painted with the letters "LTFO." What's it stand for? "Leave time for Oreos," says Trish Connolly, whose boyfriend, Devin Schmidt, drives the LTFO car. Actually, not. It stands for words I can't print here—you figure it out. There is a bit of skepticism among the drivers because the last derby event at the speedway was a "flop," according to one driver. The winner walked off with a grand total of $67.50.

Today's purse is $500 for first prize, $300 for second, and $200 for third. Brandon Kovacs of Akula Automotive is the host for today's demo; he also runs the "Mud in the Pines Mud Bog" at New Egypt. He acknowledges paltry payouts at previous derbies.

"I paid $200 out of my pocket to help you guys out," he tells the drivers pre-race. "I do appreciate you guys coming out. I'm asking you guys—tell your friends. I want to give this a fresh start. We want to grow this thing. Forget the previous thing. It's like a new regime here."

"We're trying to bring the demo back," he tells me as we walk toward the track area.

Demolition derby, so the story goes, got its start when a stock driver named Larry Mendelsohn took a turn too fast at the Islip, Long Island, speedway and rocketed 12 rows into the grandstands. That was 1958. In 1961, Mendelsohn held the nation's first demolition derby at the same track. In just two years, more than 150 would be held across the country.

"Culturally the most important sport ever originated in the United States, a sport that ranks with the gladiatorial games of Rome as a piece of national symbolism," Tom Wolfe wrote in *The Kandy-Kolored Tangerine-Flake Streamline Baby*. His description of the sport was typically Wolfe-ian: "The unmistakeable tympany of automobiles colliding and cheap-gauge sheet metal buckling; front ends folding together at the same cockeyed angles police photographs of night-time wreck scenes capture so well on grainy paper; smoke pouring from under hoods and hanging over the infield like a howitzer cloud; a few of the surviving cars lurching eccentrically on bent axles."

Bill Lowenberg, author of the book *Crash Burn Love: Demolition Derby*, describes demo as a "post Industrial Age ritual of redemption and resurrection—born, possibly, out of a drive to take things broken beyond all rational hope of repair, and let them live again." His terrific book captures, in black-and-white photos, the bravado, drama, passion, and violence of the sport, with action from Pennsylvania and New Jersey tracks, including Wall Stadium.

There are rules, of course. New Egypt Speedway's rulebook is nearly novella-length. All unnecessary glass, plastic, chrome moldings, and flammable materials must be removed. All airbags must be removed. You may not re-weld any frame or body seams. Some type of air cleaner must be used. No open carbs will be allowed. Original gas tanks must be removed completely. My favorite rule: "Just because it is not mentioned in the rules, it does not mean you can do it. Call with questions."

Minutes before the start of the New Egypt demolition derby, Brandon Kovacs and Robert Lane address the drivers. Don't be an asshole. No teaming up on people, no sandbagging in the corner.

Someone blasts an air horn, and the cars start grinding, roaring, and wheezing their way to the dirt infield. Then the crashing and smashing begin, drivers gleefully doing legally what you can't do anywhere else—destroy someone else's car.

The revving engines sound like a legion of rogue lawnmowers or belligerent buzz saws. A comic book about demolition derbies would contain a lot of *POW*, *SLAM*, *BONK* speech bubbles. Smoke rises from the much-trafficked dirt, and cars are often locked in unmoving embraces. One car sits immobile near the railing as if say, I've had enough. There is a nonstop spinning of wheels and grinding of gears. Finally, silence.

Two cars, locked together, are the last ones running. Wesley Lane, in the Cotton Candy car, is the winner. Norman Lane, in the black Punisher car, is second.

"He made the last move," Lane says of Lane. "I couldn't move." DeSantis finishes third and laments over a dead battery.

"This car absolutely would be first place if not for that dead battery," he says.

I ask Amy, in her purple 2001 PT Cruiser, what happens to the car now. "Probably scrapping it," she replies.

"It still runs," Norman Lane Sr. says.

"I didn't have reverse most of the time," she counters.

"But you were running," Lane says.

"I think the hose is shot," she adds.

There's a fair amount of trash-talking afterward. "I snapped his strut off—did you see that?" one driver says with relish. The drivers winch their cars onto waiting trailers. Most of the drivers intend to race in the demolition derby at Wall Stadium the following month. DeSantis's car looks like it drove off a couple cliffs, but he insists it will be there at Wall Stadium.

"This was my win," he says, still thinking of what might have been. "Ask the guys. If the battery didn't die . . ."

FROM BUTTZVILLE TO BIVALVE AND BEYOND

THERE ARE WINSOME, WACKY, AND weird town names all over the country—Peculiar, Missouri, anyone?—but New Jersey may boast more oddball town names per square mile than any other state.

Mizpah, Shellpile (and its next-door neighbor, Bivalve), Shamong, Shirley, Loveladies, Miami Beach (yes, it's in New Jersey), Buckshutem, Vienna, Cologne, Daretown, Leektown, Ho-Ho-Kus, Manunka Chunk.

Othello and Zion, New Egypt and Georgia, Smoke Rise and Sea Breeze, Jacksonville and Jerseyville, Mount Misery and Mount Hope, Retreat and Aura.

Upper, Middle, and Lower.

Norma, Beverly, and Dorothy.

And let's not forget the greatest New Jersey town name of all time. We are referring, of course, to Buttzville. The hamlet, part of White Township, Warren County, is not much to look at—one church, one transmission repair business, a scattering of homes. Oh, and one legendary hot dog stand—Hot Dog Johnny's, a charter member of the New Jersey Hot Dog Hall of Fame (which I just created) with Rutt's Hut in Clifton, Hiram's in Fort Lee, and Boulevard Drinks in Jersey City.

Call this chapter my homage to New Jersey geography, its rich and sometimes eccentric history of town names and places. Paisley, Purgatory, Ongs Hat, Mount Misery, Bedbug Point, Mosquito Landing Road. Comical Corners? That's no joke; it's the name for the intersection of three roads just north of Pemberton Borough.

But back to Buttzville. John Kovalsky opened Hot Dog Johnny's in 1944. He died in 1994 in a car accident right outside the business. His daughter, Pat Fotopoulos, now runs the stand on Route 46. The hot dogs are OK, but no other hot dog joint in the state beats Hot Dog Johnny's for scenery—it's along the Pequest River, with a shaded dining area out back and swings for the kids. It's a popular stop for bikers in the summer, and I've lost count of the number of North Jerseyans who've fondly recalled family road trips there as children.

The best thing to wash those hot dogs down with? Buttermilk. It's a Hot Dog Johnny's tradition! The town is named after Michael Robert Buttz, who settled here after buying a grist mill and house. Babe Ruth loved fishing in the Pequest, and Thomas Edison was a frequent visitor to Craig's Store.

The store is gone and so is the Buttzville post office, which had been located in a gas station. Close behind Buttzville in the colorfully named category is Bivalve, part of Commercial Township, Cumberland County, so named because of the once-booming oyster industry.

Not far away is Miami Beach, in Lower Township, one of several developments to spring up in the real estate boom in Cape May County in the 1920s. The streets are Florida-themed: Miami Avenue, Jacksonville Avenue, and Tampa Avenue, among others. Manunka Chunk may sound like a candy bar, but the hamlet, along Route 46 in White Township, is from the Penunqueachung Indian term *hill at the boundary*. King Cole Grove, now closed, was an ice cream stand / snack bar and a popular roadside stop.

All these colorful place-names are more than just dots on paper with a euphonious trill or thrill. There's history in these neglected nooks and crannies of Jersey. Mount Misery, along Route 70 in Burlington County, is not a mountain at all, with an elevation of no more than 100 feet above sea level. It was once home to a sawmill. Workers complained about the bad weather, worse roads, and evil mosquitoes, giving the town its name.

I always crack a smile when I say Ho-Ho Kus, in Bergen County. There are many explanations for the town's name. No, none of them have anything to do with Santa Claus. The most accepted, according to the town website, is that the word derives from the Delaware Indian *Mah-Ho-Ho-Kus*, a Delaware Indian term meaning "the red cedar."

Tranquility, along Route 517 in Green Township, Sussex County, more or less lives up to its name. The Tranquil Valley Retreat Center is located there, but so is Pub 517, a popular bar. Newfoundland, in Jefferson Township, Morris County, is distinguished by the old train station ticket office and a red caboose. The ticket office can be seen in the movie *The Station Agent*.

Loveladies, part of Long Beach Township, Long Beach Island, is named after Thomas Lovelady, a hunter and sportsman in the 1700s. Shamong, along Route 206 in Burlington County, is best known for the Pic-A-Lilli Inn and its wings. The Indian word *Shamong* means "place of the horn," but the township is likely named after a former name for Indian Mills, according to *Sign Posts: Place Names in History of Burlington County, New Jersey*, by Henry H. Bisbee. (I have place-name books and guides for most New Jersey counties; they make for fascinating reading.)

I'm not sure the resident deer population is happy about the name Buckshutem, part of Commercial Township, Cumberland County. The 3,500-acre Buckshutem Wildlife Management Area is home to sparrows, bobolink, turtles, frogs, and other species, but still . . .

Georgia is in Monmouth County (the Georgia Road Schoolhouse is the oldest remaining schoolhouse in Freehold Township); Vienna is along Route 46 in Independence, Warren County; and Rio Grande is along Route 9 in Cape May County. I remember stopping at the Rio Grande post office to ask where the old Rio Grande cemetery was. They hadn't heard of it. Actually, it was right around the corner.

That way to Shellpile and Bivalve

Route 40 might be my favorite Jersey road, and its most colorfully named town is Mizpah, home to Uncle Dewey's Outdoor BBQ Pavilion.

Road maps (remember those?) are still dotted with dizzy, ditzy names. Double Trouble and Quaker Bridge (the Pine Barrens hamlet, not the mall), Newfoundland (the one in Passaic and Morris counties, not Canada) and Woodstock (where the epic 1969 concert was most certainly not held).

Henry Charlton Beck, the unsurpassed chronicler of small-town, back-road New Jersey, wrote about such places as Shades of Death, Snufftown, Little Ease, Bedbug Hill, Recklesstown, Fooltown, Pasadena, and many more in his books, *Tales and Towns of Northern New Jersey*, *The Jersey Midlands*, *Forgotten Towns of Southern New Jersey*, and others. Beck was a quirky soul—an

Episcopal minister and sometime newspaper columnist—and his books (published by Rutgers University Press) are must-reads for anyone interested in a New Jersey that every year seems to fade a little more into the past.

Long-gone New Jersey place-names have their own happy history.

Caviar, in Cumberland County, was once the center of a bustling sturgeon roe industry. Freight trains would carry the catch to the rest of New Jersey and the nation.

Paisley was one of the more memorable, if short-lived, chapters in Burlington County history. In the late 1800s, H. A. Freeman of New York City had a grand vision: a resort community deep in the Pines. Streets were laid out, and 30 homes and a music hall were built. The town was described as "Little Paris in the Pines." But the development went bankrupt. Guess "Paris in the Pines" wasn't a catchy enough come-on.

Timbuctoo. Shiver-De-Freeze. Skunktown, in Hunterdon County. Not to be confused with Skunk's Misery (who names these places anyway?), a long-gone settlement in Salem County.

You won't find any of those towns and places on a current state map. Pity. But they tell the story of New Jersey as evocatively as any history book.

WHAT KIND OF DISHWASHER WEARS A ROLEX?

"WAIT UNTIL YOU TRY THE sauce," the Mad Cuban says, pointing at the innocuous-looking sauce on our table at La Tinajita in West New York. "You're going to be appalled."

The sauce, which tastes like watered-down Hunt's (this is not a compliment), is not as horrible as Carl Ruiz makes it out to be. The tasty bread it's meant to be dipped in is quite good, so just eat the bread, forget the sauce, and wait for the Cuban pizza. The pizza is Chicago deep-dish by way of Havana—or more accurately, Tampa—and it's better than that legendary Chicago deep dish I tried 10 years ago in the Windy City mostly because of the chorizo topping and the mix of cheeses: mozzarella, Muenster, and Swiss.

"Bakery next?" asks Ruiz. When you're on a tour of Bergenline Avenue and vicinity in West New York and Union City, you don't say no, especially to a Food Network star. You don't know exactly where this tour is going to end up, but that's half the charm. Ruiz, 44, has appeared on several Food Network shows, especially with network superstar Guy Fieri—*Guy's Grocery Games* and *Guy's Ranch Kitchen*, plus *Carl's World: Restaurant Therapy*.

The chef who goes by the nickname of the Mad Cuban also appears on *Opie Radio: The Podcast* (the initial episode about Opie visiting Carl in the cabin in the woods where he lives is a riot). Ruiz has come a long way since his Passaic Catholic Regional High School and Collegiate School days. He was born in Passaic; the family later moved to Clifton.

"My parents didn't want to put me into a public school because they knew I would turn into an arch-criminal overnight," he says of the former. Of Collegiate School, he says, "That's where I met real arch-criminals; all the kids there were kicked out of other schools."

When Carl was 14, his grandfather looked at him and said, "Your mother and grandmother keep telling you you're special. You're not. Your [older] brother is special."

Grandpa's advice: learn how to cook or go fix refrigerators. Ruiz picked the former. Wise choice. He attended culinary school in New York. "From there, it was working, working, working," he says of a succession of restaurant jobs.

His first "real" job was working under Steven Santoro at the acclaimed restaurant Dish in Clifton. Ruiz, still a teen, worked there a year for free; he considered it an internship.

"One day, Steve looks at me and says, 'Did you get your Christmas bonus?' 'No.' He says, 'What do you mean?' I say, 'I'm here for free.' 'You're not one of my employees?' 'No.' 'You're one of my line cooks, right? What do you mean for free?' I said, 'Intern.' He brings me up to

The nation's best Cuban sandwich, according to Food Network personality Carl Ruiz, can be found at La Pola, West New York.

the office, asks [the co-owner], 'How long have you known this?' 'He didn't ask for anything.'" Ruiz laughs. "I got paid from that moment."

He became a vagabond cook, working in Italy, France, Switzerland, then returning to New York City to work at Frank's Seafood on City Island and a Pop Burger in Manhattan. One day, Mick Jagger walked in and asked for owner Roy Liebenthal; Ruiz made Jagger a milkshake.

Ruiz became a restaurant consultant and earned good money doing it. "Whenever you had a problem with your restaurant, I fixed it." He would often be on the books as a "dishwasher" because owners didn't want his staff to know what Ruiz was really there for—to revamp the entire operation. Ruiz wore a Rolex; at one restaurant, the chef, convinced the watch was a knockoff, asked, "What kind of dishwasher wears a Rolex?"

Then 9/11 happened, and the New York restaurant industry took a nosedive. "The whole business just stopped," he says. He lost 12 friends from the Windows on the World during the terrorist attack. He needed to get out of New York and accepted a job to help open a restaurant at a ski resort in Switzerland. You could actually ski through the restaurant. He told the restaurant group, "This is the dumbest idea I've ever heard in my life. I'm on my way."

He returned to New York, worked at a restaurant there, and somehow ended up on Prince Edward Island and another restaurant. He met Marie Riccio; the two would later get married and open Marie's Italian Specialties in Chatham—Ruiz was the cook (the two later divorced). They opened a restaurant in Madison but ran into opposition from the start—"the building inspector just didn't like us." The restaurant was open for six months, but then Ruiz decided he had had enough and walked away.

He was working at a New York City restaurant when everything changed. Fieri had appeared on *Food Network Star*, which premiered in June 2005. He was in the running for top prize in the second season.

"He's walking down the street [after the show taping]," Ruiz recalls. "I said, 'You're going to win the whole thing.' He goes, 'No, I'm not.' I said, 'I'll make you a bet. If you win, you come to dinner on me.' He wins; that night, he shows up. My manager says—remember this is before Guy was famous—'There's some spiky-haired guy, leather jacket, says he knows you.'"

Fieri and Ruiz would go out for drinks later and, still hungry at 3 a.m., would head over to West New York for some steak sandwiches. Fieri got a six-episode commitment for his own show on the Food Network, and he asked Ruiz if he would visit several of his restaurants in California that "need attention."

"Straight nepotism," Ruiz says, laughing. "I was his friend." Ruiz would best 15 other chefs and win the championship of *Guy's Grocery Games*.

"This is when they knew they had to deal with me; that opened the door to a lot of stuff." He once judged a cookie challenge where kids were the cooks. Apparently, Ruiz was too honest with his opinions; several kids started crying.

"I said, 'I'm sorry, I thought this was a competition,'" he says, laughing.

The Cuban pizza at La Tinajita has been dealt with, and Ruiz goes outside for a cigarette break. The first stop on the "tour" was La Pola in West New York, a diner-like hole-in-the-wall that makes, according to Ruiz, the country's best Cuban sandwiches. You should have seen the Twitter firestorm when I posted photos; the city of Tampa and the mayor of St. Petersburg, plus scores of insulted Floridians, took offense—the nation's best Cuban sandwiches couldn't possibly be found in New Jersey. Didn't matter that Ruiz had eaten 500 or so Cuban sandwiches in his life and had visited many of the places suggested by the aggrieved folks in Tampa and Miami. The Cuban sandwich, he told me at La Pola, "wasn't designed for Cubans. It was designed for tourists in Cuba. As tourists started coming into Cuba, the Cubans said, 'We've got to make sandwiches the Americans like. What do they like? Mustard. What else do they love? They love that sweet ham. And Americans put cheese on their sandwiches. What cheese can we get that we don't have to refrigerate? Swiss.'"

And that, according to Ruiz, is how the Cuban sandwich was born. It's time to head to Cuban Bakery in Union City, the last stop on our tour. Ruiz, who somehow doesn't have a website, is rabidly active on Twitter, by turns accomplished chef and charming bad boy (there often is a shot of bourbon or bottle of Corona in his posts). He loves driving and eating his way around New Jersey, visiting longtime favorites (Rutt's Hut in Clifton, Sorrento Bakery in East Hanover), or checking out new places.

"You can get better food [here] than you can in Miami," he says brashly. "South American, Central American. Asian markets—just down this road is Mitsuwa [Marketplace, in Edgewater], one of the best Asian markets I've ever been in my life. South Jersey—fried fish, clams, all that. New Brunswick, when I want Indian food. Parsippany, Edison . . . there's everything here." At Cuban Bakery, he orders an empanada, a sugar donut, and a *cortadito* (espresso mixed with warm milk) that I sample and immediately order for myself.

"I think supermarkets in New Jersey have great donuts—am I crazy?" he says. He's opening a Cuban restaurant called La Cubana (Cuban woman) in New York in early 2019.

"It's a lot of work just finding the cooks who want to do it. Chefs now, they want to be famous before they're good. I had a guy, he says, 'Chef, I'm looking for this much money. Have you seen my Instagram account?' I was like, have a good day." After the Manhattan restaurant, he'd like to open a restaurant in New Jersey called Carl's Honest Food.

"Straightforward food," he says of the latter. "Every day in the food business, I fall in love with the honesty of certain places. Where the attitude is not built into them. There's not this pre-manufactured coolness. There's no focus group. I come from a world of contrived restaurants."

What will he be doing five years from now?

"Five years from now, if I'm still alive, I've got my own restaurant, I'm out of media, out of TV, just winding down and cooking. Basically, what I started doing. Instead of being part of the world, I want to be a part of watching it go by. My whole goal is to go backward."

Advice he'd give to those dreaming of becoming a chef?

"Do it free for six months. If you can cook for free for six months, then still love it, welcome aboard. But if the first day you walk in and put on whites and expect a big paycheck, you're not going to make it. There are a hundred sacrifices to being a chef that people don't talk about. Being a chef is hard work and poverty. We're servants. If you don't like serving people, then don't do it."

Author's note: Carl Ruiz passed away in September 2019. This book is dedicated in his honor.

STRAIGHT OUTTA CAMDEN

THERE'S A BULLET HOLE IN the window just above the Coors Lite sign, Zombie Killer beer in the cooler, a seething mass of meat and onions on the compact grill, Straight Outta Camden T-shirts behind the bar, and a grinning donkey's head (sculpture, not the real thing) just inside the door.

It's 10 a.m., and there's exactly one customer inside Donkey's Place in Camden, a grizzled man in his 50s wearing a ski cap, a half-empty cup of beer in front of him. Hey, whatever gets you through the night—or morning. To the right of him on the bar are giant jars of pickles and hot cherry peppers. Photos of boxers decorate the wall just above a shelf of vintage beer bottles, including long-gone Camden Beer. An American flag is draped across the brick exterior, a copper-colored awning hides that bullet hole from the outside, and consider yourself lucky if you can grab a space in the miniscule parking lot.

Donkey's Place—part dive bar, part sports memorabilia museum, part cheesesteak paradise—as much a part of the city's lore as Campbell Soup and His Master's Voice. Weekdays, the bar technically doesn't open until 10, but owner Rob Lucas is there at 8 sweeping the floors, and if he recognizes a person wanting to get in earlier, "they'll get in," he says. It's also open on the first Saturday of each month at 7 a.m. Then Donkey's transforms into a day-long party, with customers, many of them seniors, rocking dance moves that might have better been performed decades earlier.

Leon Lucas started it all. He was a lean, mean, jug-eared, fighting machine who was the U.S. amateur light heavyweight champion in 1928 and a member of the U.S. Olympic team in the 1928 Olympics in Amsterdam. After his boxing career was over, he decided to open a bar in Camden in 1947, in the space on Haddon Avenue formerly occupied by the Parkside Athletic Club, a speakeasy.

Why a bar and not, say, a pizzeria?

"Doesn't everyone want to open a bar?" Rob Lucas replies. "Back then, Camden was nicer than Cherry Hill." It would be called Donkey's Place because that was the nickname Lucas acquired as a boxer; his punch was likened to a kick from a donkey or mule.

The bar back then "straddled the boundary between predominantly Polish Whitman Park and largely Jewish Parkside," according to a recounting by Henry Szychulski and Camille Tesman-Huddell in *Camden County Heritage* magazine. Initially, roast beef sandwiches were the big draw. Then Lucas met someone who developed a mix of spices that worked well with cheesesteaks.

As a teen, Rob worked here peeling onions—"that was pretty much it," he says. The place has scarcely changed over the years. Same bar, same back dining room, same scale ("Your 'wate and fate'"), with a faded Parkside Athletic Club sign on the steps leading to the basement.

"I don't think anything's changed in here ever," he says. "Maybe the drop ceiling."

On the dining room wall is the old Donkey's Place sign—a donkey framed by palm trees. A longtime customer came into possession of it when the sign was replaced; Lucas bought it back from her for $50 "and a box of cheesesteaks." Also on the wall is a mural of a desert scene, complete with camels and palm trees. Why a desert?

"They painted it like that so people would feel thirsty," Lucas explains. It doesn't seem like Donkey's regulars would need any incentive to drink.

He points out initials carved into the bar—Bob and Elsie (his dad and mom)—and pulls out a scrapbook of photos taken by his dad in the '80s; the customers are young and old, black and white, and they all are smiling, preening for the camera.

The most prized memorabilia in the bar is a pair of boxing gloves belonging to Sugar Ray Leonard signed for the Girl Scouts of America. There are photos of Jersey Joe Walcott and, naturally, Lucas.

In the scrapbook is a letter from prison from a Robert Johnson, who also submitted some of his professional artwork—an owl perched in a tree for Halloween, a colorfully creepy jester. Johnson is long since out of jail and "still comes in here," Lucas says.

His dad, Bob, passed in 2015, and Rob took over the business. He didn't mess with the cheesesteak recipe, the meat (rib eye), or the poppy seed roll (Del Buono's), but he added stuffed cherry peppers and doubled the amount of meat on the cheesesteak, from 4 to 8 ounces, making the $9 cheesesteak a drippy, gleefully greasy monster. Good luck holding it in two hands. He also beefed up the craft beer selection, which accounts for such bottled and canned brews as Zombie Killer, Persian Lime Gose, and Lagunitas Lucky 13. On tap, stalwarts such as Coors and Heineken stand neck and neck to 7 Mile Nitro Porter, Ludlam Goats Go to Hell, Tonewood Samso, and other Jersey craft beers.

"When I took over, the most exotic beer we had was Corona," Lucas says, laughing. Business received a big boost in 2015, when the late Anthony Bourdain proclaimed Donkey's the best cheesesteak in either Philly or Jersey, and in 2018, when it appeared in the ABC sitcom *The Goldbergs*.

The place may be low-rent, but this is one dive bar active on social media; on the bar's Facebook page, Donkey's fans pose with T-shirts in faraway places—Germany, the Isle of

Donkey's Place is both dive bar and cheesesteak paradise.

Skye, Netherlands, Iraq, China, Japan, Thailand, even Lake Kickapoo, Texas. You can buy those T-shirts at the bar, along with hoodies as well as shot and pint glasses. There's even a Donkey's Place food truck, a regular at area fairs and festivals.

First-time visitors get their bell rung. No, really. You identify yourself as a newbie, one of the girls will ring the ship's bell under the register. Be warned: it makes a serious clanging racket. Rob Lucas's brother, Joe, owns Donkey's Place Too in Medford—same cheesesteaks with none of the gritty wonder of the Camden location. Has Rob ever thought of relocating Donkey's out of Camden?

"You definitely think about it," he says. "But we're staying."

My 33 Favorite Bars in New Jersey (besides Donkey's, of course)

Alibi Room, Waterford Works. A sprawling dive bar on the White Horse Pike, with a sedate front bar and a plastic-enclosed outdoor bar where you can smoke. The pole behind the bar? Patrons and bartenders—male and female—have been known to take a twirl on it. At the Alibi Room, you never need one; if someone calls asking if you're around, owner Jude Wisner's answer is always the same: I didn't see him! Good pizza, even better *zeppole* braids.

Andy's Corner Bar, Bogota. Cozy little bar, great craft beer selection. It started a block away as Bell's, then Jerry's Oval Bar, moving to its current location in 1999 in what used to be a massage parlor. Customers? "Teachers, doctors, plumbers, lawyers, truck drivers, Wall St. brokers, musicians, electricians, and artists hang out here. There's no pretensions, and no ***holes!" according to the website.

Annata Wine Bar, Hammonton. New Jersey's blueberry capital is an up-and-coming dining destination. There's Mary's Café; Marcello's; Apron Café; the Funky Cow; the annual Red, White, and Blueberry Festival; Tomasello Winery; and Annata, a wine bar / restaurant in a former auto parts store. There are 150-plus carefully chosen vintages at all price levels. Recommended dishes: the gnocchi and the braciole.

Blue Monkey Tavern, Merchantville. Never heard of Merchantville? It's next to Pennsauken. The Blue Monkey, once the high-end Collins House, is now a craft beer haven with an impressive, eclectic selection. Great burgers; they don't need ketchup or onions or cheese or anything else to appreciate.

The Boat House, Lambertville. The state's most peculiar bar, a two-story house at the end of an alley with enough nautical decor for a cruise ship and one delightfully odd policy: you can't stand up. All patrons must be seated on the chairs or couches. No standing at the bar either. If there's no room, wait in line outside. Try to grab a seat upstairs; it's like being in someone's delightfully odd attic. There's no food, but you can't beat the atmosphere, or location, in one of the state's most charming small towns.

Catherine Lombardi, New Brunswick. Located above the heralded Stage Left Steak restaurant in downtown New Brunswick, Catherine Lombardi boasts Italian fine dining and a dizzying variety of cocktails on the encyclopedic drink menu. The restaurant hosts an ongoing Spirits Project; every Thursday at 6:30 p.m., a bottle of a luxury spirit is opened, and 1-ounce pours are sold at cost. The bar was one of 60 semifinalists in our NJ's Best Bar Showdown. For my visit, they named a drink after me—the Peat Genovese, with Boomsma Genever Oude, fresh lemon juice, cinnamon syrup, chamomile syrup, honey, and Laphroig Scotch whiskey. It was quite tasty—and I'm pretty sure it's not on the menu anymore.

Clydz, New Brunswick. Clydz has a split personality: small bar with an enormous drinks menu, dining room with an often adventurous menu in back. Clydz is known for its exotic-game dishes; you haven't lived until you've tried braised python ravioli, kangaroo loin, or duck flatbread. At the bar, ask for the special drink list, filled with drinks custom-concocted by the bartenders. My favorites: the Nutty Alexander ("Secretly the best drink on the menu," one bartender told me) and the Destroyer.

Coconut Grove, National Park. Drive to the end of the road, past marsh and reeds, to the "Grove," in a picture-postcard setting on Woodbury Creek. In the summer, as many patrons come by boat—there's ample slip space—as by car. The bar, known as the White Bridge in the '60s, is big and airy, but when it's warm outside, you want to be on the deck. Great wings. National Park? It's a borough in Gloucester County. But you knew that.

The Corner Bar, Pilesgrove. Nearly 200,000 people voted in our NJ's Best Bar Showdown. I visited 60 bars in the semifinal round, and the Corner Bar ended up #1. More dive than neighborhood bar, it's easy to find—at the corner of Routes 40 and 45, across the street from a giant Wawa and a cemetery. Free peanuts and popcorn, dollar Miller High Lifes all day every day, and surprisingly good food.

C-View Inn, Cape May. Cozy neighborhood bar just over the little bridge that links Lower Township and Cape May. Owner Greg Coffey calls it "the local storm bar" because it somehow manages to stay open even during the worst storms. Try the prime rib sandwich or the wings with the special sauce kept behind the bar.

The Deep Inn, Newark. This raffishly charming Ironbound dive bar was once a funeral parlor. From the outside, it looks grubby and grim. Inside is a cozy, well-kept locals' hangout; you don't stumble in here by accident. There's no food menu, but owners Joe and Marianne Downar put out a free buffet during football games.

The Great Notch Inn, Little Falls. A recent highway-widening project went right around "The Notch"—it would have been a damn shame to tear down the log cabin–like bar. It traces its roots to 1924, when current owner Rich DiLeo's grandfather opened the Green Chateau, where you could get beer in the bar and milk from a walk-up window. Bikers are frequent visitors, and it's one of the state's preeminent rock and blues bars. Check out the ancient cash register behind the bar; the TV is always tuned to one concert or another. Admission is always free.

Gyp's Tavern, Sandyston. I love Gyp's, perched prettily on a lake at the top of New Jersey. It's a hunter and hiker hangout; you can bring your deer in and have it weighed or write your name down in the Appalachian Trail logbook kept behind the bar. Hundreds of police, fire, and service badges and insignia decorate the walls and ceiling. The jukebox is packed with such roadhouse tunes as Big Al Carson's "Take Your Drunken Butt Home," only Big Al doesn't say *butt*. Babe Ruth once drank here and hunted in the nearby woods; there are photos of him on the wall in the couch-furnished back room. Excellent wings.

Hudson House, North Beach Haven. There are folks on LBI who've never heard of the "Hud." It doesn't announce its presence; it really is a house on a side street, and there's no big neon sign. It's cash only, there's no food or frozen drinks, and the stools are patched with duct tape. The shuffleboard board dates to the '50s, and the general atmosphere is laid-back and leisurely. On an island known for popular (and much bigger) bars and clubs, the Hud—compact, cozy, and stuck in time—stands out.

Jay's Elbow Room, Maple Shade. Lively neighborhood bar with a good craft beer selection and great lunch specials—sandwiches for a dollar from opening until 2:30 p.m. Monday through Friday. Monday's is steak sandwich; Tuesday, chicken steak; Wednesday, roast pork; Thursday, hot roast beef; Friday, beer-battered chicken filet. Just off Exit 4 on the turnpike, Jay's is a great alternative to all the chain restaurants/bars in the area.

Johnnies, Boonton. You've got to love a place that hosts a turkey bowling competition in the parking lot around Thanksgiving. You read that right—bowling with frozen turkeys. Johnnies looks like just another house on the block, but inside is a locals-packed dive bar with a colorful background; the building has been home to a speakeasy, funeral parlor, and soda factory. There's a shuffleboard table, a back bar, high ceilings, and such signs as "If You're Smoking, You'd Better Be on Fire."

Krug's Tavern, Newark. An Ironbound legend and winner of our NJ's Best Burger Showdown. Frank Krug (pronounced *Kroog*) opened the bar in 1938; it is now owned by the LaMotta family (related to Jake LaMotta, the middleweight champion boxer of the '40s and '50s portrayed by Robert DeNiro in *Raging Bull*). The burgers are simple, big, juicy—and great.

Le Malt, Colonia. An upscale cocktail lounge with VIP rooms—in a strip mall? That's Le Malt, a one-of-a-kind bar that attracts a well-heeled crowd. Drinks are made table-side. Owner Saurabh Abrol, who also owns the Wine Chateau next door, visited bars as far away as Scotland and Dubai before creating the whiskey-centric Le Malt. Recommended: the VIP Cosmo (Belvedere vodka, Cointreau noir, cranberry juice, fresh lime) and the mojito (prosecco, Hennessy cognac, and mint leaves). The menu features "sophisticated" tapas; I highly recommend the lamb lollipops. A sister, members-only bar, Le Malt Royale, is in Red Bank.

Louise and Jerry's, Hoboken. The Mile-Square City does not lack for packed, noisy bars; this may be its most sedate, at least in the afternoon / early evening. It's small and narrow with a pool table in back. And the bathroom may be the smallest bar bathroom in the state. For those who keep track of such things.

Lower Bank Tavern, Lower Bank. My favorite Piney bar, a rambling retreat on Route 542, one of my favorite highways in New Jersey. It's a locals' hangout; you don't "accidentally" find the Bank. There's also an outdoor bar with picnic tables. "Do it in the Pines" says the sign outside.

Lun Wah Restaurant & Tiki Bar, Roselle. Amazing bar, a tiki-head and palm tree-decorated extravagance with blowfish-shaped lights, bamboo walls, umbrella-topped drinks in giant bowls. The only thing missing is a floor show with Polynesian dancers. Tropical-themed drinks include mai tais, the Hawaiian Sunrise (vodka and lime juice), and the Chi-Chi (coconut milk, vodka, and juices), but for full effect, order the Volcano, a drink for two with fruit juice and light and dark rum that is set afire at your table.

Motts Creek Inn, Galloway. Ignore the greenheads, the bane of southern Shore living, and enjoy the views—marsh, water, and sky, the kind of beautiful, spare emptiness typical of bayfront towns from New Gretna south. Minutes away is the Oyster Creek Inn in Leeds Point, another scenic waterfront retreat with good seafood.

Murphy's Tavern, Rumson. When we held our NJ's Best Bar Showdown, it was amazing how many people in the immediate area had never heard of Murphy's. It's a bar in a house, and you could easily drive right past it. The bar dates to Prohibition, when it was frequented by rumrunners working the nearby Navesink River. There's a dartboard and a killer jukebox (Johnny Cash to Neil Young and everyone in between), great bartenders/owners, and surprisingly good food. Try the truffle pizza or the pork roll fries.

Old Log Cabin Inn, Columbia. Rollicking roadhouse with the Delaware River right across the street. The bar is a trip—tilted floors, animal heads on the wall. The pizza, made in an adjoining room, is really quite good.

Park Tavern, Jersey City. Looking for a great bar away from the hustle and bustle of downtown Jersey City? The Park Tavern—cozy, cave-dark, no sign outside—is the place. And no blaring music, just a muted jukebox. Great burgers here, cooked on a small grill and big on flavor.

Pattenburg Inn, Pattenburg. I once lived up the hill from this bar, but that's not why it's on this list. It's a country roadhouse with a great live band reputation, superfriendly staff, and really good food. The cheesesteak is the best within miles, and the wings are first-rate. It's the kind of place where you immediately feel at home even if there's a raging snowstorm outside, which happened when I was last there.

Plank Road Inn, Secaucus. What was Chris Rock doing atop a table at the Plank Road Inn in 1985? Stand-up, what else? The comedian performed for $30 and taxi fare back to New York City; his photo is on the wall of this bar, minutes from the Meadowlands. The house shot is the Shooter McGavin, after the character in *Happy Gilmore*, a summer-smooth concoction of Jameson, sweet tea vodka, peach schnapps, and lemonade. The Frankenstein wings—so named because they combine three sauces—are recommended.

Riverside Inn, Cranford. Act like you belong and just call it The Dive. No other bar in Jersey lives up to its name more. A steady cast of regulars—from 20-somethings to grizzled characters like owner Pete "Jake" Jacobs—can be found here. The building once housed a Model A dealership, speakeasy, and flower shop. Hurricane Irene flooded the town and the bar; the bar became known as the "River Inn Side." The food is better than you might expect; cook John McCarthy does wonders in his cramped kitchen. Recommended: the prime rib; it's ridiculously good. The day's specials are colorfully drawn on paper plates and hung behind the bar.

The Shepherd and the Knucklehead, Haledon. The Shep is the best craft beer bar in New Jersey, for my money. The bar's name comes from the title of a novel by owner Chris Schiavo about "the duality in man." His son, Joe, runs the bar, which boasts a staggering 90 craft beers on tap. Good food here; try the burger, the Angus sliders, or the open-faced steak sandwich.

The Stewed Cow, Hoboken. Whiskey connoisseurs will be wowed at this cozy bar well off Washington Avenue, Hoboken's main drag. There are 100-plus American whiskeys, from the affordable to the astronomical. A 2-ounce pour of cult whiskey Pappy Van Winkle 15-year Reserve will set you back 200 bills. I once tried a taste; it's impossibly smooth, dizzyingly delicious, borderline dangerous. Don't like whiskey? There are about 20 draft taps. The menu includes the Roadkill Platter (brisket, bacon, scrambled eggs, and biscuit, with spicy sausage gravy), or the Infamous Brunch, with a choice of entrée, plus two brunch cocktails, muffin and pastry basket, and "sumpthin' from the house for the table."

The Stirling Hotel, Stirling. Rustic roadhouse that's small and cozy in the winter and becomes a big happy lawn party in the summer with outdoor bars and picnic area. There's a moose head on the wall, oddball signs, and cozy booths. Recommended: the burgers, a blend of brisket and short rib, and the homemade chips.

Tierney's Tavern, Montclair. Great neighborhood bar that started during Prohibition as a candy shop across the street. The tavern itself opened in 1934; it was built by a group of Swedish boat-builders who also built the Great Notch Inn in Little Falls. The burgers are terrific.

Tir na nOg, Trenton. The state's most authentic Irish pub, Tir na nOg is free of the clichéd signs and posters you'll find in other Irish pubs. It's cramped and cozy and friendly as can be, and there are frequent band appearances by the likes of the Shantys, Black Brant, and the Tir na nOg Pipeband. Wander into the back room and check out the Greater Trenton Dart League action. The bar's owner is Todd Faulkner, who met his wife at a Tir na nOg in Boston.

Verve, Somerville. The slightly upscale Verve is the town's nerve center, the place in which judges, prosecutors, and just plain folk gather. One of the state's coolest hangouts is the upstairs red-lit lounge, open only on weekends, where movies often play on a screen.

THE MOST BEAUTIFUL COLOR OF ALL

THERE IS NO MORE SPECTACULAR New Jersey color than the blazing crimson of a cranberry bog in the fall.

"Should I come up through Black Rock?" Stephanie Haines asks someone on her phone. We're in her pickup truck heading to Blueberry Hill Bog, part of the 1,400-acre Pine Island Cranberry Co. in Chatsworth. The state's largest cranberry operation, it was founded in 1890 by Martin L. Haines, a Civil War captain who planted cranberries in what was known then—and now—as Hog Wallow.

Right now though, Stephanie is not sure she's taken the right road to the bog. What we're on isn't a real road, just a perilously narrow dirt way between ditches. I'm thinking the state should give driving lessons here to make sure motorists can drive in a straight line. The road we're initially on doesn't get us from point A to point B, so Stephanie circles back and tries another way.

"The weird thing about this place is that you can't get there from here," she says, smiling. She's the social media coordinator for Pine Island, which consists of maintaining the company's Facebook page and giving tours to the legions of pesky reporters who want to visit during harvest time.

The bogs here all have names. Telephone Hill. Panama. Otter. Otis. Black Rock, after the 1955 movie *Bad Day at Black Rock*, starring Spencer Tracy. Stephanie and several of her siblings have bogs named after them too. Her dad, William Haines Jr. II, great-grandson of Martin L. Haines, runs the operation. Haines is one of 700 cranberry growers in North and South America who are part of the Ocean Spray cooperative, formed in 1930. The co-op's first product was jellied cranberry sauce, a staple of Thanksgiving Day dinners 90 years later. The co-op's other high-profile product: cranberry juice cocktail. By 1980, Ocean Spray surpassed $500 million in sales; by the 1990s, sales exceeded $1 billion.

New Jersey is the third-largest cranberry-producing state, after Wisconsin and Massachusetts. In 2016, cranberries brought in nearly $28 million. About 400 million pounds of cranberries— Pine Island produces about 30 million of that total—are consumed in the U.S. every year, 20 percent of those on Thanksgiving. If you strung together all the cranberries produced in North America annually, they'd stretch from Boston to Los Angeles more than 565 times. Think about that the next time you say something unkind about cranberry sauce.

Workers at Pine Island Cranberry Co. funnel cranberries toward a waiting truck.

Cranberry growing is a complicated business, and more high-tech than you might think. A Rutgers University research station near Chatsworth develops the varieties; the Lee family, another large grower with bogs adjacent to Pine Island, grow the cuttings. It takes three years for the rooted cuttings to take hold, five years for full production. Bogs are flooded—the water comes from the aquifer, plus the Oswego and Wading Rivers—at harvest time, when the berries float to the surface.

"A lot of people think that cranberries grow under water," according to the Ocean Spray website. "Makes sense, since we usually see the berries floating on top of the water. But, what we're seeing is actually the result of wet harvesting. The bog is flooded with up to 18 inches of water the night before the berries are to be harvested. The growers then use water reels, nicknamed 'eggbeaters,' to churn the water and loosen the cranberries from the vine. Each berry has a tiny pocket of air that allows it to float to the surface of the water."

The berries are then corralled by workers into a funnel and into a waiting truck, the berries cascading skyward and sideways. Leaves and debris go the other way into a smaller truck. The berry-filled trucks barrel down to an Ocean Spray receiving station five miles away. There, cranberries are dispersed into holding tanks, then sorted on conveyor lines. They're tested in a lab for firmness and color. Years after being planted, those cranberries finally end up in your cranberry sauce or juice. Those are just the basics. About 200 rented beehives work their pollination magic in the spring. Bog moisture levels are checked on iPads. Workers are constantly on alert for the berries' number-one enemy—tundra swans, which love a weed known as red root that grows alongside cranberries.

"They'll swoop in, pull up the root, tear up the bogs," Stephanie explains.

For Eastern Indians, the berries were known as *sassamanesh*. The Lenni Lenape called them *ibimi*, or "bitter berry." Native Americans believed in the berry's medicinal value; they would make poultices from the berries to draw poison from arrow wounds. Early German and Dutch settlers started calling it the "crane berry" because of the flower's resemblance to a crane's head and bill.

"We're the biggest [grower]," Stephanie says as we walk down a pathway between the bogs. It is a warm, sunny afternoon for late October. I am tempted to lie on the ground and take a nap, framed by the brilliant blue skies and that astounding crimson.

"The Lees are sixth or seventh generation," says Stephanie, breaking me from my reverie. "They may have started before us. With us, it's fourth generation currently running the farm. Fifth generation coming up." Her dad is a member of the Ocean Spray board of directors. The family also owns 250 acres of bogs in Chile; those berries are sold in Brazil and Europe.

"It's roughly the same latitude, the same soil," she says. "It's not as humid. It's not as big an operation down there, but it's coming along." At Hog Wallow, Pine Island employs 30 people year-round; another 50 are added seasonally, many of those from Puerto Rico.

What makes the Pine Barrens perfect for cranberries? "The sandy acidic soil," Stephanie replies. "It's one of the few things that can grow in it. You've got your pine trees, cranberries, and blueberries, and that's about it."

Later, I drove home, heading straight to the supermarket to pick up bottles of Ocean Spray mixed berry and tropical juices. Damn, were they good. I'd like to think that little bit of Jersey inside made them special.

EAT WHERE THE TRUCKERS—AND BONO—EAT

"CAN I GET THREE PANCAKES with a side of . . ."

"No pancakes," says the waiter. He looks at the compact grill toward the end of the diner, where three men move with practiced ease, flipping burgers, adding toppings, wrestling baskets of fries from the deep fryer. "We busy right now."

"French toast . . ." he begins.

"Then I'll have French toast," I say.

"No pancakes, no French toast," he says quickly. "Anything else you can have."

"Bacon and egg on a hard roll?" I venture.

"Yes."

Whew. I felt like I was in the breakfast version of John Belushi's classic "Cheeseburger Cheeseburger . . . No Coke, Pepsi" routine on *Saturday Night Live*.

It's noon at the Truck Stop Diner in South Kearny, and the retro diner is packed and pulsing with life. Truckers, construction crews, warehouse workers, locals—people who look like they belong here. You don't stumble upon this diner by accident. It's tucked into the Jersey Truck Stop on Truck 1-9, a couple shouts away from the other Route 1, the Pulaski Skyway.

"*Opa*," a waitress greets a customer in a booth.

"*Opa*," he replies.

"*Opa, mi amor*," she sings happily.

English, Spanish, and Greek are spoken interchangeably here. Next to the grill, owner Sam Kolokithas ladles soup from stainless steel urns—today's choices are chicken noodle, clam chowder, and something called Spanish soup, made with yucca, beef, corn, cilantro, celery, and potatoes.

The soup bowls are enormous, the biggest I've seen in any diner. They seem to fit right in here—nobody in the lunchtime crowd seems about ready to go on a diet. Even the healthy-sounding "avocado toast" is a heaping mountain of avocado, egg, and greens, with the toast under there somewhere. There is a laminated menu, or you can look up and read the old-school white-lettered menu on the wall, with such diner standards as liver and onions, corned beef hash, hot open roast beef, and chicken soup. Taped-to-the-wall photos show zesty quinoa salad and cheeseburger sliders. There's a photo of a berry-topped waffle with the caption underneath

Lunchtime, Truck Stop Diner, Kearny

reading, "Chicken salad sandwich special." The phone rings constantly; the diner does a booming business in takeout orders.

There is a TV atop the Pepsi display case, another facing the other direction atop the Snapple case. "Want to know if your partner is cheating?" a commercial asks. Boxes of Celestial Seasonings tea are stacked to the right of the coffee urn. On the counter, a Cabot sour cream canister does duty as a straw holder. Oranges glisten from a cylindrical holder; plastic-wrapped cookies beckon from a cake holder. Boxes of Timberland boots ($75) and caps ($5) sit atop a cabinet just inside the door.

The guy sitting next to me wears enough bling to open a jewelry store—two chains around one wrist, a watch and two bracelets on the other, with rings on every finger of his left hand.

A woman at the counter with a bowl of chicken soup tells a waitress, "I can't wait until happy hour. Two more hours."

I want to live her life. It's only 12:57 p.m.

A half-hour later, the lunchtime rush over, and Kolokithas sits down at the counter next to me. I ask what's changed in the past 25 years; that's the last time I saw him.

"Nothing has changed," he says. "Same old diner." The diner, built by the Kullman Car Co. in Harrison, once stood at the corner of 50th Street and Eighth Avenue, across the street from the old Madison Square Garden. Then it was called the Arena Diner. In 1948, it was moved across the river to South Kearny, New Jersey's least-scenic, least-sexy mile-and-a-half square, a gritty industrial netherworld wedged between the Passaic and Hackensack rivers, home to the state's largest wine and spirits distributor (Fedway), truck terminals, warehouses, a helicopter charter company, one prison, one municipal utilities authority, and one very large truck stop—the Jersey Truck Stop, where the Truck Stop Diner is located.

Kolokithas bought the diner in 1989; the interior is classic diner—booths, swivel stools, stainless steel—although the vintage chrome exterior was recently bricked over.

"It was falling apart," Kolokithas explains.

"What kind of soups do you have?" a customer, Colleen Brady, asks Artie Sapikas.

"Clam chowder, chicken noodle, Spanish soup," he replies.

"Is it spicy?" she asks of the latter.

"No. Real good."

"I also need a grilled chicken salad, but no tomatoes, no cheese, no croutons," Brady says. She works for T3 Expo, which builds trade shows at the Jacob Javits Convention Center and other venues. The company just moved its offices nearby, and Brady has become a steady customer of the diner at the corner of Hackensack and Scout.

"I love these guys," she says. "Nice guys. Good food. Good soup." She spots a waitress and says, "This lady is great too. What's your name?"

"Stella," the waitress replies.

"That's your name; what about your number?"

"911," Stella says, laughing.

Next to me, Khurram Malik takes healthy bites of his cheeseburger. He's the owner of RN Shepherd Express, a trucking firm at nearby Raul's Truck Repair. His buddy, Giovanni Rogo, has also ordered a cheeseburger.

"We're in love with the cheeseburger," Malik says, grinning. It's 1:25 p.m. and quiet, and I see pancakes making an appearance on the grill. Hmm, should have waited longer.

Now's a good a time as any to talk about the Truck Stop Diner's most famous customer since, well, maybe forever. Bono and The Edge from U2 stopped here in the summer of 2018.

Apparently, the band was shooting a video nearby. There's a photo of Bono and The Edge on the diner's Facebook page. Few noticed the post; there's just one comment, someone asking, "What did they eat?" It's not clear what they did eat, but there's something on the grill right now I definitely don't want to eat—a grilled cheese sandwich with a mountain of bacon stuffed inside.

Kolokithas tells me he bought The Point Diner in Fairview 10 months previous. Why did he buy it?

"It was for sale," he replies. The Truck Stop Diner is South Kearny's only diner now that the Skyway Diner, several blocks away, has closed for good. Situated right under the Skyway, the diner made an appearance in *The Sopranos*.

Sapikas rubs his eyes; he's been working since five in the morning. Ten more minutes, and he's off. His uncle, Pete Sotirhos, owned this diner in the 1970s, then bought the Skyway Diner. Sapikas and Kolokithas both worked at the Skyway.

"I do the soups, the specials here," says the weary-looking Sapikas.

Dominick Tullo walks over and says hi. His father, Alex, owns the Jersey Truck Stop. "This place is unique, one of a kind," Dominick Tullo says.

"Everybody knows this place, all over the United States," Kolokithas adds. "Truckers from Texas, Louisiana, California, Maine, Wisconsin, Chicago." He smiles. "Everyone knows the Jersey Truck Stop."

The Best Diners in New Jersey
(Apart from the Truck Stop Diner, of course)

Nothing says Jersey like a diner. We are the diner capital of the world, after all, with about 600 diners. Outside, chrome shining in the sun; inside, a warm, welcoming atmosphere, with swivel stools and booths. Waitresses who call you "honey," menus the size of telephone books, and endless fills of coffee. Here are my favorite diners around the state.

Americana Kitchen & Bar, East Windsor. The Americana Diner ended up as the state's top diner in an epic 55-diner road trip I did for *Inside Jersey* magazine in 2013. I don't want to know how much weight I put on during that mission. The Americana remains in the upper echelon of Jersey diners; the owners also run the Skylark Diner and the Pines Manor, both in Edison. Neither the Skylark nor the Americana will remind you of classic diners with their sleek, modish looks, but the Americana's menu is expansive and the food quite good.

Angelo's Glassboro Diner, Glassboro. Maybe the state's quintessential small-town diner, Angelo's Glassboro Diner opened in 1946 and has scarcely changed since; they still don't take credit cards. A dozen stools, a half-dozen tables; the menu, like the diner, is compact, but the food's hearty and cheap. Scrapple—that pork-scrap side dish once described as "everything from the pig except the oink"—is available too. Roast turkey, liver and onions, tapioca: the diner itself seems comfortably stuck in some cozy time warp.

Broad Street Diner, Keyport. The winner of our NJ's Best Diner Showdown on nj.com, the Broad Street Diner is a cozy small-town diner that serves up a tasty slice of '50s kitsch with a thoroughly modern menu—smoked brisket hash and eggs, Cajun shrimp penne, and my favorite dish, the chocolate *babka* French toast.

Chit Chat Diner, Hackensack. The Chit Chat Diner is part of the new wave of diners: big, shiny, around-the-clock restaurants with staggering menus, well-stocked bars, and dessert cases big enough to feed an army or two. Any diner that can encompass coconut-crusted French toast, pastrami tacos, *banh mi*, *lomo saltado*, and Tex-Mex meatloaf is a diner to be reckoned with.

Colonial Diner, Woodbury. The state's liveliest diner waitresses can be found here, a wise-cracking crew who will liven up the dreariest day. They're constantly playing jokes on each other; one likes to squirt customers with fake mustard—yellow string in a mustard squeeze bottle. Oh, and the food's good.

Maurice River Diner, Maurice River. Admit that you can't find Maurice River, the town, on a map. The Cumberland County diner serves up all the diner standards, with an emphasis on seafood and Italian dishes. Recommended: the South Philly steak and the Greek salad. Good homemade cheesecake too.

Mustache Bill's Diner, Barnegat Light. A diner that wins a James Beard Award must be doing something right. Mustache Bill's won a prestigious America's Classics award from the James Beard Foundation in 2009, the first diner to receive the honor. Current owner Bill Smith started working at what was then Joe's Barnegat Light Diner in high school, buying the diner in 1972. And yes, he has a mustache. The food is neither boring nor predictable; try the shrimp tempura, potato skin omelet, the caramel apple rose tart—and the scrapple.

Park West Diner, Little Falls. The Tick-Tock Diner, on Route 3 in Clifton, is North Jersey's best-known diner; but I like the Park West, minutes away, more. Co-owner Jimmy Douranakis's rags-to-riches diner story began on a park bench in New York City in the early '70s; Douranakis, recently arrived from Greece, had nowhere else to stay. He eventually ended up at the Park West, where he was a dishwasher along with John Stoupakis and Peter Kapalos. The three now own the Park West, best-known for its fresh, creative salads.

Park Wood Diner, Maplewood. Best diner chicken pot pie? No contest—it's at the Park Wood Diner. The owner is Pete Kikianis; he's the guy going from table to table, making sure everyone's happy. "Diners are a beautiful thing," he says. I won't argue with that. The salads here are among the best in any Jersey diner—try the Perfect Illusion or the warm goat cheese salad. There's a nice outdoor patio in the summer months.

Point 40 Diner, Monroeville. I love my Greek salads, and one of the best at any Jersey diner is the Greek salad at the Point 40. Crispy greens, plenty of feta, and kalamata olives make it special. Snapper soup is a South Jersey tradition; the one here is musky, murky, and memorable. I remember the upturned noses when I brought a container of the stuff into a staff meeting.

Pompton Queen Diner, Pequannock. Chicken taverna! The broiled half chicken, enlivened with Mediterranean herbs and spices, is reason enough to visit the Pompton Queen. It's another big, bustling diner on a busy highway. Save room for the delicious desserts.

Ponzio's Diner, Cherry Hill. South Jersey's best-known diner, especially with Olga's in Marlton torn down. Ponzio's has its devotees and detractors, but this sprawling diner served up excellent food in multiple visits during our NJ's Best Diner Showdown several years ago. Highly recommended: chicken pot pie, blackened prime rib, stuffed French toast. And I've stopped in for their cinnamon bread more than a few times.

Reo Diner, Woodbridge. Donald Trump's photo is on the wall at the Reo, along with Chuck Norris and other celebrities who have stopped in over the years. It opened as the Hy-Way Diner in 1928; the name was changed to Reo after the vintage car of the same name drove past the diner one day. Good breakfast, and for dinner, try the double pork souvlaki: two hunky kabobs of nicely seasoned meat.

Roadside Diner, Wall. Maybe the most striking-looking classic diner in New Jersey, with its red railroad-style roof, yellow awnings, and a stainless-steel sheen. The diner can be seen in John Sayles's 1983 movie *Baby It's You*. Dig the sliding glass door and the tiny bathrooms.

Salem Oak Diner, Salem. That's not just any tree across from the Salem Oak Diner—that's the Salem Oak, New Jersey's most famous tree, 600-plus years old and reason alone to visit the Salem County town (the tree fell down in June 2019). I wrote about the diner 20 years ago for my book *Jersey Diners*, and nothing has changed. Soft-blue booths, coatracks, and jukeboxes (which, alas, don't work) make for a classic atmosphere. Try the Chicken Athena, with fresh spinach, tomatoes, feta, olives, and garlic in a white wine sauce and served over linguine. For dessert: the rice pudding.

Sparta Classic Diner, Sparta. It may remind you more of a stylish casual restaurant than a diner, with its light-brown decor, cylindrical yellow / burnt orange light fixtures, and linen napkins at each booth, but one look at the menu tells you this is a diner all the way. You can get nachos and calamari, spinach and artichoke dip, charred lamb salad, short rib burger, and albacore tuna melts. They pride themselves on their burgers—there are 11 on the menu, including one with Taylor ham, provolone, jalapeños, sautéed onions, and disco fries.

Summit Diner, Summit. This classic diner was the first chapter in my book *Jersey Diners*, and it holds a special place in my heart 20 years later. If I had to take a diner first-timer to one Jersey diner, it would be the Summit, with its curved roof, wood paneling, padded booths, and a grill where you can see, smell, and practically touch your food. Order a slider (not the usual mini-burger but a Taylor ham, egg, and cheese sandwich) and a cup of coffee, and drink in one of the state's essential food experiences.

Tom Sawyer Diner, Paramus. The Tom Sawyer replaced the Paramus Diner, which opened in 1974 and burned down in 2006. The Tom Sawyer is more stylish, upscale restaurant than classic diner. The menu is sprawling, with everything from omelets, burgers, and chicken clubs to Mediterranean chopped steak, sesame ginger salad, and French toast Napoleon. Highly recommended: the spinach pie and the sirloin steak sandwich.

Tops Diner, East Newark. Yes, East Newark is a real place, and unlike Newark, it's in Hudson, not Essex, County. Tops Diner, which opened in 1972, started small, but today, it's a huge, shimmering, neon-lit palace with lines often out the door and high-quality food. It's not a 24-hour diner, as many believe; they shut down several hours each night. The amount of food served here is staggering: about 4,000 pounds of chicken and 2,000 pounds of burgers each week. The menu is enormous, with un-diner-like items such as tomato and goat cheese bruschetta, Maui fish tacos, and a short rib grilled cheese. Try the meatloaf.

Tropicana Diner, Elizabeth. The diner formerly known as the Betsy Ross Diner and Camelot Diner became the Tropicana in 1991. Island-themed murals provide a tropical decor, and the menu effortlessly combines Greek, Latino, and traditional American dishes. The most popular breakfast item is the Colombianita, a mountainous mix of rice and beans, *huevos puericos* (scrambled eggs with scallions and tomato), arepa, ahi sauce, and avocado slices served with either steak or chicken. Yeah, good luck finishing it. Another belly buster: the *grande picada*, with chorizo, chicken and pork *chicharrón*, tostones, baby back ribs, potatoes, yucca, and tomatoes. My favorite dish, though, is the *churrasco*, skirt steak served sizzling on a plate.

Tuckahoe Family Diner, Tuckahoe. It doesn't much look like a diner from the outside, but inside, this 1945 Silk City diner exudes considerable retro charm. Diner pancakes are often forgettable—believe me, I've eaten enough of them—but the ones here are homemade, hearty, and first-rate. Excellent burgers too—big, fat, and juicy.

Victoria Diner, Branchville. A stainless-steel beauty at the top of Jersey, the diner started as the Wayside Diner in Rockaway and was trucked here in the 1950s, where it was later known as JD's and the Five-Star Diner. Those expecting just pancakes and burgers will be surprised by a menu that includes Tuscan roast pork loin, chicken Napoleon, bayou blackened steak, and the mixed berries French toast. Thinking about the latter makes me want it for breakfast tomorrow.

BOOST!

THE FIRST DISCLAIMER ABOUT THIS chapter is that if you live outside Burlington or Camden counties, you've probably never heard of Boost!

That's Boost!, the lemony cola pride of Riverside, not Boost, the nutritional drink from Nestle. No two drinks, or companies, could be more unalike. Boost! is New Jersey's most peculiar beverage, a dark-reddish syrup that is mixed with water to produce a cola drink that is as distinctive as it is unclassifiable. Many describe it as a "flat cola," others as a lemony iced tea. The more fervid Boost! believers have referred to it as "liquid crack."

The label on the 64-ounce bottle of Boost! calls it a "concentrated blend of citrus fruit syrup." That doesn't do the drink justice either.

Before we decide what it is, and isn't, let's talk to Dan McDonough. He's president and general manager of the Boost! Co., headquartered in Riverside. McDonough seems to be the drink's biggest—sorry—booster.

"We are a premium product. We pride ourselves on that," he says, adding, "There's no one who enjoys their job more than me."

"Ben Faunce's drink since 1913," proclaims the labels on the Boost! bottles. Benjamin Rice Faunce opened a pharmacy in Riverside in the early 1900s. Along with his medicines, he developed a drink he called Tak-ABoost, "a concentrate that could be dispensed as a non-carbonated soda [or could be] mixed with seltzer water or milk, served in milkshakes or used as a topping for ice cream," according to a booklet prepared for the company's 100th anniversary. This is where things get complicated; bear with me. Tak-ABoost was trademarked in 1913; the company was known as the Boost Co. Tak-ABoost stores popped up in Pitman, Blackwood, Palmyra, and other South Jersey towns. In 1950, a family dispute led to Randle B. Faunce (Ben's son) and his son, Randle N. Faunce, plus E. Lester Stockton (Ben's adopted son) and his son E. Lester Stockton Jr., forming Drink AToast Co.

In 1950, Boost Co. sued Drink AToast over the formula; Drink AToast won that battle. Boost Co. went bankrupt in 1957, with Drink AToast acquiring the Tak-ABoost trademark. In 1962, Drink AToast built a manufacturing plant in Riverside, still in use today. In 1996, Drink AToast won a lawsuit against Mead Johnson and their Boost product for copyright infringement. In 1997, members of the Faunce family took over the company, and Drink AToast started trading as the Boost! Co.

Believe it or not, that's the short version of the drink's history. McDonough started at the company in 1987, just after high school, as a driver and salesman, taking over as general manager in 2004 and president / general manager in 2006. He introduced more flavors and Boost! in slushie form. He and Boost! go way back. He attended St. Casimir's in Riverside. Every Friday was pizza and Drink AToast day. There are just seven year-round employees. A grand total of two drivers are added in the summer.

"They do everything," McDonough says of his staff. "We bottle it, deliver it, market it. It's a well-oiled machine." Each week, his drivers make deliveries to 600 stores, "the majority of them mom-and-pops, some Acmes," McDonough notes. The jugs can be found in dozens of convenience stores throughout Burlington and Camden counties—there's a list on the company's website—but the bulk of the company's business is in Boost! slushies.

"The product is best in slushie machines," McDonough says. "I've been running with it since 2004. It's been going crazy." The first Boost! slushies were sold by Frank Casciella, owner of Frank's Deli in Beverly. He had a ledger—"thick as a Bible"—where he wrote down customers' orders.

Boost! central might be the Krauszer's in Riverside, where there are no less than 12 Boost! machines. "They do an unbelievable amount of Boost! every week," according to McDonough. Boost! slushies are fabulous; I tried one at UMMM Ice Cream Parlor in Burlington City. The drink seems to have more punch and sweetness than the mix-your-own bottle form.

Matt Garwood, owner of UMMM, may be an even bigger fan of Boost! than McDonough. "We've had Boost! from day one," he says of his delightfully retro ice cream parlor / soda fountain. "We're about the only place where you can have it on tap [mixed right on the soda gun with syrup and water], and one of the few places where you can get slush and nonslush.

"It's definitely an acquired taste—and not in a bad way," Garwood adds. "Some people say it tastes like flat Coke or iced tea." He calls it "the nectar of the gods" and "somewhat like the best-kept secret in the area."

How much Boost! does he drink? "Way too much."

Manny Monteiro, owner of the Shamong Diner, is another big Boost! fan.

"It's great; it's amazing," he says of Boost!, which is sold at the Pine Barrens Store, his market/deli next to the diner. There's even a Boost! sign out front, by the side of the road. To me, the drink tastes like an uncarbonated lemony iced tea. Definitely different, kind of addictive. I kept a cup of Boost! slush in my freezer for nearly three months before defrosting and sampling it (don't ask why). It tasted as fresh and delightfully oddball as the just-made version.

"It's a lot like Coca Cola syrup; we're more like them, not Pepsi," McDonough explains. "It's a cola base; that's the best way to describe it to someone who doesn't know what it is . . . a

A Boost! fountain drink and slushie at UMMM Ice Cream Parlor, Burlington City

lemon-and-lime base with a hint of cola." There is a secret ingredient, which of course he wasn't about to reveal to me: "The main flavoring of the product I know. What it is, I can't tell you. It's just me and one family member on the board who know [the formula].

"We've never changed any ingredients," he adds. "It's made the same way it's always been." Four parts water, one part Boost! is the recommended ratio for the syrup, "but around here, it's three to one," according to McDonough "It's thicker, stronger. Around this area, they like it strong."

In 2013, Boost! was honored as one of a handful of third- and fourth-generation businesses by Southern New Jersey Business People at an awards night.

"They told us what our odds were in staying in business this long—7 percent," McDonough recalls. "Now we're in our 105th year. The odds have gotten worse." So why hasn't Boost! expanded its reach?

"It was, how big do you want to get? They [the Faunce family] did what they did and did it well. I think they thought if they got big, they'd have more problems." McDonough attends many local parades with a Boost!-labeled 1929 Model A that took him two years to restore. Boost! may be an unknown quantity in North or Central Jersey, but good luck finding anyone in Burlington County who didn't grow up with it. Throughout the years, many high school reunions in the area have made sure to have bottles of Boost! on hand for those syrupy trips down memory lane. The 64-ounce bottles of syrup are shipped worldwide; the most popular state it's ordered from is Florida, where retirees sure do miss their Boost!

"We have the most loyal customers in the world," McDonough says. "They're the best sales-people we have."

IF YOU HAVE A HEARTBEAT, PLEASE CALL

MOHAMMED RAFI, VOTED "INDIAN CINEMA'S Greatest Voice" and whose funeral procession in 1980 drew 10,000 mourners, and Lata Mangeshkar, who once held the Guinness World Records honor for most songs ever recorded by a single artist, are singing, "O tere naino ke mai dip jalaunga" from the 1972 Hindi movie *Anuraag*, about a man who falls in love with a beautiful blind woman he meets while walking on the beach. The song is followed by "Hum tum gumsum raat," from *Hum Shakals*, a 2014 Indian romantic comedy film. Then it's time for a commercial.

". . . major brands like Ashley, Lazy Boy," a female announcer says brightly. "Living room, dining room, bedroom and more. And mention EBC and get a free gift."

"Yes, you heard that right," an energetic male voice jumps in. "Get a free gift now. US Brands Furniture, 4115 U.S.-1 South, Monmouth Junction, New Jersey. US Brands . . . the biggest sale, sale. See you there!"

There's one constant about commercial radio—if you don't have advertisers, you won't stay on the air long. Alka Agrawal and her husband, Arvind, know that as well as anyone. EBC Radio (1170 AM WWTR), headquartered in South Brunswick, is the largest and oldest Indian radio station in the United States, with about 500,000 listeners, but that doesn't mean there haven't been lean years.

"We give thousands of smiles on the radio, but at the end of the day, we have tears in our eyes [because advertising is not enough]," Alka says. "Why are we not smiling?"

The smiles have far outweighed the tears, though, since 1999. At the time, the two would rent space twice a week at WCNJ Hazlet. They would stash 300–400 CDs of Indian music in their car trunk. But why start a radio station?

"The thought came; the opportunity came," she says.

"An investment," he adds. In 2002, they switched to a commercial frequency—WTTM. "It was like an atom bomb," recalls Arvind, eyes alight. "Everyone started listening."

"When we started, [we had] maybe 10,000 listeners," she says. The number reached 100,000 in 2004. In 2005, the station (ebcradio.com) switched from 1680 AM to 1170 AM.

"Now we have a half million listeners," Alka says proudly. In 2011, they bought the frequency, making the two the "first to own an Indian frequency in the U.S.," according to Alka. India Aboard calls EBC "the largest and oldest channel for the South-Asian community in North

Kushi, one of the RJs at EBC Radio

America . . . With more than 30 radio hosts, the station brings together a rich mix of personalities and perspectives, on music, news, debates, local community events and more." The hosts are called RJs (for radio jockeys). They include Kushi, who is on from 8 to 10 a.m. two days a week. (The RJs go by first name only.)

"I've been with Alka for 10 years," Kushi says. "This is my passion. EBC is my second family. And I love to talk to people." She picks a weekly theme for conversation. "This week I picked, 'If someone at work takes credit for what you did, do you say something or do nothing?'"

The hottest singer right now, she says, is Atif Aslam, a male Pakistani singer who has recorded many chart-topping songs, including "Dekhte dekhte," which has earned nearly 200 million views on YouTube.

Gia, who is on from 1 to 3 p.m. weekdays, likes to talk "about love and the heart."

"I play Bollywood music, and I choose a quote of the day, [with] two opposing things, like smile and agony," she explains. She tells listeners: "If you have a heartbeat, please call." None of the station's 25 RJs had prior DJ experience, according to Alka. She said she was looking for "passion" when hiring.

Eighty-five percent of the programming is music, and it's all Bollywood, all the time. Bollywood is, of course, the Mumbai-based Hindi cinema, where music reigns supreme. The top movies of 2018 included *Raazi*, which a news website described as a film "that evoked nationalism in every heart . . . [with] a powerful script that left us in tears when the film ended."

EBC is generally on from 5:30 a.m. to 8:30 p.m. Zahida, the station's office manager, makes sure everything is running smoothly. Iselin's Little India, along Oak Tree Road, is the center of commerce for Indian Americans in New Jersey, but the station's reach goes well beyond Woodbridge and Edison.

"Plainsboro, South Brunswick, Princeton Junction, Hamilton—so many Indians," says Arvind, wearing black suspenders over a blue-checked shirt. "South Brunswick—35 percent [of the population] are Indians." Their listeners are also from Bangladesh, Sri Lanka, and Pakistan.

"A lot of Caribbean people—a lot of them are of Indian descent," Arvind points out. About 80 percent of their advertisers are small businesses; the remainder are hospitals, car dealers, and banks. Every two weeks, on Saturday, an Indian doctor from St. Peter's University Hospital in New Brunswick comes in to do a medical-related show.

"When we started, radio in India was not that popular," says Alka, who serves on the Asian Indian Chamber of Commerce board of directors. "People said, 'Who listens to radio?' Now radio is very big in India."

In 2004, an Indian Ocean earthquake and tsunami that killed 230,000 people in 14 countries brought New Jersey and New York City news crews to the station. They wanted to interview Alka on the disaster's effect on the local Indian community—had they heard from friends and family overseas?

"We were connecting people," Alka says. "No one knew how severe it was. It happened in the night. One woman came in [who] was worried about her family; she could not reach them." Listeners started calling the station, many offering information on what towns and regions were affected.

"Thousands of listeners were getting relief," she says. Callers mailed in checks to the station for relief efforts.

There are several minutes of commercials, then it's time for more music—"Palki pe hoke" (from the Bollywood movie *Khalnayak*) and "Jhoum jhoum," sung by Himesh Reshammiya, from the 2006 Hindi comedy *Tom, Dick and Harry*. Arvind sits in his office, a satisfied smile on his face. A station employee brings in cups of tea.

"[Whether] you are 5 years old or 90 years old, uneducated or a rocket scientist, poor or a billionaire, you listen to EBC Radio," he says.

AT THE DOCK OF THE BAY

THE FIRST THING I LEARN about Dave Tauro is that it doesn't take much to get him wound up.

"Did you see the story about the bunker?" says the manager of the Belford Seafood Co-op as I walk into the store and introduce myself. I have no idea what story he's referring to, but no matter; he's off and running on a mild-mannered rant that takes in government regulation and fishing restrictions and fisheries councils and commissions whose members have no clue what they're doing along with "tree huggers" seemingly trying to put commercial fishermen out of business, and why don't they actually talk to real fishermen to see what's going on?

"They go out with all their gear, never fished a day in their life—they read a book," Tauro fumes.

Seafood co-ops are one of the little-known, underpublicized treasures of the Jersey Shore. There's Belford Seafood Co-op, on Raritan Bay in that section of Middletown and the Fisherman's Dock Cooperative in Point Pleasant Beach. Belford and Point Pleasant are also two of the state's six major commercial ports, along with Atlantic City, Cape May, Port Norris, and Barnegat Light, the latter home to Viking Village. It sounds more like a theme park gone medieval, but Viking Village's 50 or so boats haul in about 2 million pounds in each of three main categories (scallops; long-line, which include tuna and swordfish; and net, which include bluefish and monkfish). Those are numbers fishermen working Belford's 20 boats can only dream about. And it's doubtful Belford will ever go Hollywood like Viking Village did. One of the latter's boats, the *Lindsay L*, was used in *The Perfect Storm*.

Brag all you want about the "fresh fish" at your local supermarket, but fish doesn't get any fresher than at a seafood co-op or port. Fish offloaded from boats are put on sale in the adjoining market; bulk amounts are delivered to restaurants. The Belford Seafood Co-op's Facebook page tells you what fish are available each day and the price.

> Beautiful jumbo sea bass $7.00 pound
> Large whiting $2.50 lb
> Jumbo porgies $2.99 pound

The co-op's customers always are quick with questions:

> How are the clams today? Sweet and white? Looking for 100 or so of top necks or smallest chowders.

A commercial fishing boat pulls away from the Belford dock as seafood co-op manager Dave Tauro (right) watches.

Tauro's response:

> Paul, I always have clams if you want, to Pacific size. Just call me and I will get them

How's that for customer service?

"Our dock survives on fluke in the summer; we make our money on fluke," Tauro says in the co-op's market. He is awaiting the return of the *Dutch Girl*, about four hours out from the dock. He's been the dock manager for five years and general manager the past three months. This is no newcomer to commercial fishing.

He started clamming when he was 12. He made more money the summer he was 14 than both parents put together. "My mother wanted to know why I had [several thousand] dollars in my closet. She thought I robbed a bank or something."

As soon as he was old enough to drive, he bought a '68 Camaro, then a '71 Camaro. "That and women is where my money went," he says.

> We [have] live lobster 7.99 lb
> Fresh shrimp 10.99 lb
> King whiting 2.50 lb
>
> Customer: ShopRite has lobsters $5.99 lb
>
> Tauro: ShopRite lobster is new shell. Buy one of my lobsters and then go buy
> one from ShopRite and you'll see what I mean

On my second visit to the co-op, Gina Graham, Dave's girlfriend, is working. A cigarette dangles from her mouth as she ties up a boat dockside. Surprisingly, neither she nor Dave are big fish-eating fans. Ling and tilefish are the only two Gina favors.

"A steak is going to win that fucking battle," she says, laughing. Inside his riotously cluttered office, Dave is on the phone with a wholesaler. A co-op regular needs oysters. "You have 100 oysters for me? I don't care what they are as long as they're the cheapest." He kneads two golf balls in his hand as he talks. Four cigarette butts are crumpled in an ashtray. Next to the ashtray is an unopened bag of Drake's Apple Fruit Pies. There's a tangle of cords for phones and lights, a folded piece of legal pad paper, a brass sextant, wrapped chocolate in a jar, an adding machine, and a box of 20 Mule Team Borax (to keep the dock surface clean).

> Today is opening day of crab season for us!!
> We have bushels available!
> #1 Males $90.000 bushel
> #2 Males $60.000 bushel
>
> Customer: Belford crabbers: Good luck to all, kick ass

The long-held stereotype of the commercial fisherman, I wrote in a 2013 profile on Viking Village, was "that of a bearded rogue who squandered his earnings in the nearest bar once his boat landed. These days, commercial fishermen are drug-tested, and immature or irresponsible behavior gets you tossed off a boat faster than a deckhand in a hurricane."

"I don't think we get the respect we should," Peter Dolan, the burly captain of the boat *Ms. Manya* told me at the time. "There are no fools around here anymore. These are clean-cut guys with families." Same goes for the fishermen who work out of Belford. Roy Diehl has been with the co-op 35 years. He's captain of the 60-foot *Phyllis Lynn*.

Yesterday was a 13-hour day. "Half day," he says, laughing.

> Hello my name Is David Tauro
> I manage the fish store. I have a comment for a couple of those people that had questions about the fluke.
> When it comes to rules and regulations for fishing New Jersey is the worst
> Our fishing boats are told
> When we can go fishing
> How much we can catch
> We have our government come on our boats
> We have [fish & game officials] waiting at the dock when we come in
> For anybody [who doesn't] know who they are. They are police.
> So I would like anyone of you
> To tell me how much you have to go through
> TO FEED YOUR FAMILY!!!
> Thank you
> David Tauro

The fluke season runs two months at a time, with quotas each time. Reach your quota, your boat goes idle.

"We're at the lowest quota we've ever had," Diehl moans. "It's hard to keep young guys in the fishing game when there's no money to be made." In the summer of 2017, the Belford boats laid idle for a month after fishermen met their summer flounder quota a month ahead of schedule due to the Atlantic States Marine Fisheries Commission slashing the quota by 30 percent from Maine to Florida that February.

"They say there's no fish," Diehl told the *Asbury Park Press* at the time. "Well, we caught our whole summer quota in two weeks, so there's plenty of fish out there."

> I had four boats land this morning!!!!
> Seabass 6.99 lb
> Fluke 5.99 lb
> Porgies 2.99 lb
> Butter fish .99 lb
> Large squid
> Thank you, David

Most of the Belford captains are in their 60s; Diehl wonders who's going to take over when he and the older fishermen retire. His son, Roy Diehl Jr., works with him, but he's an exception.

"You don't see young guys here," says Roy Diehl Jr. "That's a dead giveaway. The writing's on the wall." Operating a boat is expensive business. A day trip may cost $600–700 for fuel and ice. If he's lucky, a fisherman will make $400–500.

"If the boat don't make a thousand bucks a day [gross], you shouldn't be out there," Diehl says. The weather's ever-changing and unpredictable. "Sometimes it's nice out; it can be 50 degrees at the dock going out, [then] com[ing] back here, you cut through ice and it's nine degrees." Talk returns to quotas, which the fishermen say are putting a stranglehold on their livelihood.

"We're limited to what we can do; we're boxed into a corner," Diehl says. "We're hanging on—barely. We never had to worry about making a living before now."

YOU'RE IN THE BREW ARMY NOW

FINDING BACKWARD FLAG BREWING IN Forked River is a bit tricky. Make the turn off Route 9 onto Old Shore Road, drive past the Bolt Bin, make a right onto Challenger Way, and look for the warehouse-looking building and a Backward Flag sign. If you hit the Master of Bargains, you've gone too far.

Backward Flag—so named because the flag patch on a military uniform's shoulder sleeve must, according to regulations, be worn so that the star field faces to the observer's right—is one of 100-plus craft breweries in New Jersey. A new one seems to open every week. They range from Blairstown and Lafayette to Woodbury and Cape May and are housed in a colorful array of places—storefronts, bars, warehouses, storage facilities, even airports.

Some produce a handful of barrels a year; others crank out tens of thousands. The best-known include Carton Brewing in Atlantic Highlands, Kane Brewing in Ocean Township, River Horse in Ewing, Flying Fish in Somerdale, and Cape May Brewing in Lower Township.

What makes Backward Flag different is that it's the state's only female veteran–owned brewery, and it maintains a seriously low profile even for a craft brewery. Its founder is Torie Fisher; the head brewer is her partner, Melinda Gulsever. Torie's favorite non–Backward Flag beer: Left Hand's Milk Stout Nitro. Melinda's: Neshaminy Creek's Highwater Hefeweizen. Both served in the military; Fisher served 13 years, including two tours in Iraq, first with the First Armored Division, then with the Army National Guard, where she was a Black Hawk helicopter crew chief.

Asked if she felt in danger in Iraq, she replies, "I think anyone who says they're not scared [over there] is lying." She's a self-described Army brat who lived in Louisiana and Hawaii. She tells me she joined the military at 18, then sheepishly corrects herself—"Actually, I was 17." In high school, she dreamed of being a photojournalist or wartime photographer; she remembers flipping through the pages of *Life* magazine's year in review issue and being fascinated with the wartime photos. She then considered enrolling in art school, but her dad had some sage advice: "You know artists only make money when they're dead."

After her Army duty, she joined the National Guard. She and her now-ex-husband started home brewing, and Fisher says she started feeling "a little bored with my career."

"I knew I wanted to be a business owner; I didn't want to work for anyone anymore," she explains. Her initial idea was a brewpub, but she quickly realized she had zero restaurant or business experience—"Not a clue," she says, laughing.

During an interview, a representative of SCORE, a partner with the U.S. Small Business Association, asked Fisher, "How much capital do you have?"

Fisher's response: "What's capital?" She and her ex-husband, who is no longer part of the brewery, scouted locations in the area, none of which came cheap—$14–15 a square foot. She found a bargain—$1 per square foot, 2,100 square feet in all—in the Forked River industrial park, on Challenger Way—just steps, coincidentally enough, from the Master of Bargains, a pet supply store. She started small, with a barrel and a half; a 10-barrel system was installed in February 2018.

"We thought all of our problems were solved," she says of the increased production capacity. "The problem is, the more beer you make, the more beer people want." The brewery opened in 2015 as a bare-bones operation and remains so.

"We don't have fancy floors or a fancy bar," according to Fisher. It reminds her of what is known in the military as a "crew shack," built piece by piece with found materials. The couches, for one, came "from the side of the road." Military, police, and fire badges adorn the walls, and just inside the entrance is Fisher's Army uniform. A big board shows the results of the latest Army-Navy football game.

"Army has won the last [three] years," she says gleefully, although she overlooks the fact that Navy won the previous 14 games in the series. (Navy did win the 2019 game; the interview was conducted in 2018.) One poignant corner of the taproom is filled with photos of fallen soldiers supplied by their parents. Gold Star parents—parents of soldiers killed in action—always drink free at Backward Flag.

How much does it cost to start and operate a brewery? The initial cost for the one-and-a-half-barrel operation was about $130,000. Ramping it up to a 10-barrel operation cost another $350,000. Fisher has taken on a business partner—a veteran "with a decent access to cash" is all she will say. Backward Flag is more than just about beer; the brewery regularly hosts fund-raisers for veterans groups, and its monthly Forward Assault series of canned beers are collaborations with worthy veterans organizations in which 10 percent of proceeds go to the sponsoring organizations. Every month, 10 percent of all bartender tips go to soldier groups or organizations. Signs on the bar, across which tiny plastic soldiers march, indicate the organization of the month.

Combat Edison, an American wit or white ale, is part of Backward Flag's Forward Assault series, a collaboration with Bunker Labs (a nonprofit network of veteran entrepreneurs). I bought a four-pack of Combat Edison; it's quite good. When it comes to time to determine a collaboration in the Forward Assault series, Fisher doesn't simply tell the organization, "This is what we're going to brew." She mails them "personality questionnaires" that give the organizations a voice in the process. Sample question: "If you were a fruit, what kind of fruit would you be?"

Interior, Backward Flag Brewing, Forked River

Each month, there's a new release, "which is fun, but every month, you're jumping on a new recipe," she says with a sigh. A more recent brew in the Forward Assault series: Rugged Road Chestnut Brown Ale, a collaboration with Backpacks for Life, a nonprofit that provides support to homeless and at-risk veterans. The first can in the series was Something's Missing IPA, a collaboration with veteran activist Rory Hamill, who lost his leg while serving as a marine in Afghanistan. There are usually 10–12 beers on tap, and all are military-themed, from Oak Armored Ale (the most popular beer from day one) and Hot Brass, a habanero and lime ale, to the Valkyrie 240 IPA (named after a machine gun) and the Morning Formation coffee milk stout.

As with any craft brewery, not everything that comes out of the barrel is drinkable. "We've had beers that we've put down the drain for technical flaws," she says. Asked about other women brewers, she says, "Women who brew beer or women who are spending daddy's money?"—then diplomatically declines to say more. Female brewers are a minority in New Jersey—at last count, there were a dozen female owners or brewers among the state's 114 craft breweries (the number does not include the state's 19 brewpubs).

As a veteran, Fisher labors under a double standard. First-timers to Backward Flag notice the women behind the bar or back by the kettles and ask, "Isn't this a veteran-owned brewery?" In any event, Backward Flag is very much going forward. Fisher talks of contract brewing with River Horse Brewing in Ewing and one day opening a new, and considerably bigger, facility.

It's late afternoon, and visitors start to fill the taproom. There is a tired, resigned look on Fisher's face. "I've been here since this morning," she says. "I'm done. I want to drink beer."

24 Great New Jersey Breweries (besides Backward Flag, of course)

7 Mile Brewery, Rio Grande. Cape May County is bursting with craft breweries—Cape May Brewing, Cold Spring Brewery, Bucket Brigade Brewery, Gusto Brewing, Ludlam Island Brewery, Slack Tide Brewing—and 7 Mile, located in a strip mall across the highway from a Walmart. My favorite beer there: Se7en saison.

Cape May Brewing, Lower Township. This sprawling brewery is always on the short list in any discussion of the state's best breweries. It's the beer version of Willy Wonka: tanks bubbling, centrifuges spinning, assembly lines whirring, bottles clinking, with enough noise to rival an airport runway. Actually, it's headquartered at an airport—Cape May Airport. The brewery has come a long way since 2011, when it opened in a storage unit–sized space. They now brew more beer in one day than they did all that first year. Favorite: Geek Out wild ale.

Carton Brewing, Atlantic Highlands. Another craft beer heavyweight. The second-floor tasting room is a compact space where dogs happily camp out on the floor and humans lounge on well-worn couches or lean against the bar. The brewery opened in a turn-of-the-century brick warehouse. My favorite: Nitro Milk, a stout.

Death of the Fox Brewing, Clarksboro. They take their coffee as seriously as their beer here. Gourmet international coffee and espresso are available every day. Founder Dan Garrity, like many craft brewery owners, had home brewed for years before opening his own facility. My favorite: Stout Heard 'round the World, on nitro.

Departed Soles, Jersey City. Flights come on skateboards, and exposed ductwork provides the decor. All beers are made with 100 percent gluten-free ingredients. My favorite: Cantankerous Blonde, a terrifically refreshing lawnmower or summery beer. (Next door is Bucket & Bay Craft Gelato—highly recommended.)

Double Nickel, Pennsauken. A spacious—make that huge—taproom on Route 73. Their Core series pays tribute to five styles: Vienna lager, IPA, session IPA, pilsner, and Belgian golden ale. My favorite: Father Barrel, a rye porter aged in bourbon barrels.

Eight & Sand Beer Co., Woodbury. The brewery opened in 2016 in a former pasta factory. The focus here is on classic European session beers. Nonstop train videos play on a big screen; the brewery's name is railroad slang for "quick and safe travels." As of this writing, NJ craft breweries are not allowed to serve food (some do offer snacks or have food trucks stationed outside). You are allowed to bring in outside food, though; Bo Ne in Woodbury makes terrific banh mi sandwiches. Favorite beer: the barleywine.

Flying Fish Brewing, Somerdale. Flying Fish opened in Cherry Hill in 1996; its former facility there is now occupied by Forgotten Boardwalk Brewing. Flying Fish is known for its Exit series, based on New Jersey Turnpike exits. One of these days, I'm going to open the bottle of Exit 18 Baltic Porter in the kitchen; it's been sitting there a while. The brewery raised some eyebrows when it released a pork roll porter in 2016. My favorite: Daylight Savings IPA.

Glasstown Brewing, Millville. Head to the airport—Millville Airport—to find Glasstown Brewing; the brewery is inside the Army Air Field Historic District. Bar inside, picnic tables outside. No bands or pool tables or raucous crowds. My favorite: Super C IPA.

Hidden Sands Brewery, Egg Harbor Township. I immediately fell in love with this brewery when I tried their guava sour. There's always a sour or two on the tap list. The brewery won a first-place award at the 2018 Atlantic City Beer & Music Festival for its First Drop coffee maple porter.

High Point Brewing Co., Butler. High Point, which opened in 1996, describes itself as "America's premier brewer of German-style lagers and wheat beers." Their flagship beers include an imperial pilsner, an amber lager, an "ink black" lager, a golden lager, a blonde Hefeweizen, and my favorite, the double platinum blonde Weissbock.

Jughandle Brewing, Tinton Falls. Jughandle is one of many New Jersey craft breweries to take up residence in a strip mall; Jughandle is neighbor to a RiteAid, a bank, and a preschool. It's owned by three friends, one of whom had just finished a term as mayor of Tinton Falls before the three started hatching plans for a brewery. My favorite: Party Guy stout.

Kane Brewing, Ocean Township. One of the most highly regarded Jersey breweries, Kane is headquartered in what looks from the outside like a dentist's office. Walk through the gift shop, though, and you'll end up in the cavernous tasting room. Owner Michael Kane is partial to American-style and Belgian-influenced ales. I interviewed him at the Great American Beer Festival in Denver in 2014, where the brewery won a gold medal for its A Night to End All Dawns, an imperial dark ale that starts as an imperial stout and is transformed into a strong dark ale after 15 months in bourbon barrels.

Last Wave Brewing, Point Pleasant Beach. Last time I was here, a thunderstorm with threats of a tornado raged outside. The taproom exudes a surfer vibe, with boards on the wall. About 15 beers are on tap at any one time. My favorite: A-Frame IPA.

Lunacy Brewing, Haddon Heights. Lunacy's former location in Magnolia was one of the state's funkier breweries, an open-air bar situated past a forbidden-looking chain link fence. The Haddon location is brighter and more spacious, with illuminated beer menus on the wall. My favorite: Sanitarium Double IPA.

Magnify Brewing Co., Fairfield. Eric Ruta, Magnify's founder, says he wants to play "a significant role in magnifying the craft beer culture throughout New Jersey." The brewery is known for its IPAs, but my favorite is the Low Visibility pale ale.

Referend Bier Blendery, Hopewell. Referend Bier is one of the state's more original breweries, with all beers spontaneously fermented and aged in oak barrels. It all makes for distinctive brews. My favorite: Berliner Messe.

River Horse Brewing, Ewing. River Horse's move from Lambertville to Ewing meant the brewery had the capability to go from 9,000 barrels a year to about 80,000 barrels. Their beers are readily available throughout New Jersey. My favorite: Hippotizing IPA.

Screamin' Hill Brewery, Cream Ridge. When I stopped at this farm-based brewery during the summer, the crowd was split between beer hipsters and bikers. Sit outside at one of the benches and enjoy the pastoral view. My favorite: Habanero Ale.

Spellbound Brewing, Mount Holly. Spellbound has one of the wider distributions statewide in liquor stores; it's great walking into my local liquor store and always finding a four-pack of at least one of their beers. My favorite: Spellbound IPA.

Tonewood Brewing, Oaklyn. Tonewood, which opened in 2016, sports a cool, casual taproom. "No overcomplicated beer," one of its owners promised at the beginning, and they've held true to that. The Fuego, a cloudy IPA, is the most popular beer, but I like Chief, a pale ale, more.

Troon Brewing, Hopewell. Tucked behind Brick Farm Tavern, Troon looks more like someone's garage than a brewery. There's no formal tasting room, and only 32-ounce cans are available. My favorite: Mineralized Matrix IPA.

Twin Elephant Brewing, Chatham. Twin Elephant's tasting room is one of the more original and convivial in the state; the woodwork is all salvage, including 350 pallets and the remains from a friend's bar. The last time I was there, there seemed to be more kids—several running about—than adults. Favorite beer: Common Heritage, a hoppy saison.

Wet Ticket Brewing, Rahway. Watermelon Wheat ale is all you need to know here; it's a delightfully refreshing brew that indeed "tastes like summer," as the can proclaims. Steps away from the tasting room is Nancy's Towne House, which makes one of the state's best thin-crust pizzas.

GROWING UP UP UP

"WE'RE GOING TO GO THROUGH a quick bath," Marc Oshima tells me inside AeroFarms.

No, not that kind of bath, but a sterilizing floor pad with lime-streaked grids. All visitors to AeroFarms in Newark must walk over it—after they've put hairnets on their heads and covers on their shoes.

Vertical farming at AeroFarms

It's one of many rules and regulations at the most surreal farm you're ever likely to see. Jewelry is prohibited (wedding bands with no stones are allowed if worn under a glove). No sandals or open-heeled footwear, no dresses or skirts. When you're the cutting-edge future of farming, you need to be really careful about contamination.

AeroFarms, in the Ironbound, is a vertical farming facility. Plants grow without soil under brightly lit shelves stacked eleven high to the 30-foot ceiling of a former steel mill. If all of that sounds unlikely, you should see it in person. The facility looks like something out of a sci-fi movie, albeit one involving kale, mustard greens, and baby arugula.

The LED lighting—"proprietary design," Oshima notes—makes for "more effective photosynthesis." Plants that normally grow in 30–40 days take 12–16 days here, which would be the envy of gardeners everywhere. No need to worry about weather, weeds, pests, or pesticides; no need to break out the hose; heck, you don't even need any soil.

The 70,000-square-foot complex is just part of AeroFarms' grand vision to turn Newark into a vertical farming mecca. It may already be there. The company's R&D headquarters is on Market Street, a space that was an Urban Apparel store, then a nightclub. "When we went in there, the disco lights were still there," Oshima says, smiling. The corporate office is on Park Place; another farm is on Ferry Street, in what was once Inferno Limits, a paintball and laser tag arena. There's a year-round indoor market at the Ferry Street location from 3–5 pm.

A visit to the Ironbound facility, though, is a trip. Plants arrayed vertically instead of horizontally? No soil? And everything indoors? Is this for real?

"Everything you see," says Oshima, leading me around the farm, "is being grown for a specific customer." ShopRite is a key partner; its distribution center is minutes away.

"ShopRite puts a lot of emphasis on sourcing produce from local farms in the communities where our stores operate," Derrick Jenkins, vice president of produce and floral for ShopRite, told *Inside Jersey* magazine. "AeroFarms offers fresh produce we can source right here in Newark for our local ShopRite store." Other customers include FreshDirect, Seabra, Whole Foods, plus schools and restaurants. AeroFarms' retail line is called Dream Greens.

"They're producing these greens that taste the way greens are supposed to taste, the way I remember them tasting as a kid," Steve Yglesias, owner of Mompou, a tapas restaurant in Newark, told the *New York Times*. "There's a flavor profile that includes a wonderful nutty flavor. And if you put them up against greens from another big supplier, there's no comparison in the freshness factor and in visual appeal. They won me over."

It all started with a couple buddies from business school. Oshima and David Rosenberg met at Columbia Business School and formed a company called Just Greens in 2004. Research led them to Ed Harwood, a former Cornell professor, who was working on aeroponic farming. Harwood, now AeroFarms' chief science officer, developed the reusable cloth (made from recycled water bottles) that is now used as a soil substitute. Seeds don't sit in water but are misted with a mix of water, oxygen, and nutrients. LED lights provide the right intensity, spectrum and frequency each plant requires for photosynthesis.

AeroFarms uses 95 percent less water than traditional farms, and crops can be harvested 30 times a year instead of two or three, as at a normal farm.

"We're managing the entire process from seed to plant under one roof," Oshima explains. Why Newark?

"We've had a working farm at Phillips Academy for eight years now," he begins. The charter school students harvest their own greens from an AeroFarms unit in their dining hall.

That's part of it. Oshima was a Jersey guy who headed up marketing for the Food Emporium and was on the marketing board for the Food Bank for New York City. AeroFarms is dedicated to going into underserved neighborhoods and eliminating food "deserts." Newark was a prime candidate.

Oshima, Rosenberg, and Harwood found a willing business partner in Newark. Mayor Ras Baraka and his team have been "tremendous," according to Oshima. The company received a community development grant from the city and a $1 million grant from the Food and Agricultural Research Foundation. AeroFarms has "close ties" with Rutgers at Newark and New Brunswick. In another partnership, 19 employees have been added to the workforce through a reentry program. AeroFarms' original plan was to add 78 jobs to the community; the number was at 120 in late 2018, with 40 percent of the workforce living in Newark.

The company's financial partners include several venture capital firms, plus Goldman Sachs, Prudential, and IKEA. In 2017, IKEA, renowned chef David Chang, and the ruler of Dubai—Sheikh Mohammed bin Rashid Al Maktoum—invested $40 million in AeroFarms. Dubai has become a vertical farming hot spot. Crop One Holdings and Emirates Flight Catering plan to build a 130,000-square-foot vertical farm—the world's largest—in Dubai. The greens will be used for in-flight meals on Emirates airlines. Infarm in Berlin builds modular farming systems that can be found in local supermarkets, and Plantagon International is designing vertical farms in Sweden and Singapore. There are an estimated 150 vertical farms in Japan, although none on the scale of AeroFarms' Newark facility, which will soon be eclipsed in size by another AeroFarms, in Camden, with twice the growing size of the Newark farm.

There's another vertical farm in Newark—Radicle Farm, which operates out of an 8,000-square-foot greenhouse in Branch Brook Park that hadn't been used in 20 years. Radicle grows a number of microgreens, including kale and spinach. Its founders are Tony Gibbons, former maître d' at the Gramercy Tavern in New York City, and Jim Livengood, a former grant writer at Liberty Science Center in Jersey City. Their Chef's Selection blend combines red and green romaine lettuce with bitter mustard greens, peppery arugula, and mizunas for what an *Inside Jersey* story described as a "fiery mixture of piquant flavors."

AeroFarms has grown 300 different leafy greens so far. "There are about 50 varieties of leafy greens growing right now," Oshima points out.

A cartload of watercress rolls by. Maybe it's the lighting or the dazzling weirdness of it all, but the greens on the shelves look so fresh and inviting, I want to grab a fistful and take them home.

"We're creating a new category of food where flavor and nutrition are at the forefront," Oshima adds.

AeroFarms was named one of *Fast Company*'s most innovative companies of 2018. And *Inc.* magazine named AeroFarms one of its 25 Most Disruptive Companies of the Year, given to those that employ "groundbreaking ideas and ambitious plans for bringing them to market."

Back in the company vestibule, I discard the hairnet and shoe coverings and walk back to my car, shaking my head. Was all that real?

SERENADED ON NEW JERSEY'S OFFICIAL TALL SHIP

Brandy good for sailor men,
Brandy O.
Early in the morning,
Brandy O,
Early in the morning,
Give us a drop of brandy.
Brandy good for sailor men,
Brandy O.

A TALL SHIP GLIDES, SERENE and stately, on Delaware Bay. Gulls swoop by on the starboard side. There is the faintest of breezes on this late summer morning. A four-member a cappella group, the Johnson Girls, are singing sea chanteys, some happy, some sad, some just a bit bawdy. They are Deirdre Murtha, Bonnie Milner, Joy Bennett, and Alison Kelley, and they've been together for 21 years.

At the ship's wheel is Capt. Johann Steinke, who makes his living piloting tall ships.

"Ladies and gentlemen," he tells his passengers, "we're about to go sailing. And to prove it, I'm going to kill the engine." So begins another cruise on the *A. J. Meerwald*, New Jersey's official tall ship.

The boat, launched in 1928, was one of hundreds of schooners employed during the heyday of New Jersey's oystering industry. Bivalve was its capital, a thriving town of homes, hotels, restaurants, meat markets, lumberyards, and a post office. Trolley tracks and a railroad line ran through town. The Bivalve Hotel entertained guests.

They're all gone now; diseases by the names of MSX and Derma largely wiped out the oyster industry over the years, though a handful of oystermen remain. Once-thriving Shellpile, just down the road, is practically a ghost town. An overpowering sense of history and loss hangs over both hamlets like early morning mist.

The *A. J. Meerwald*, which can be found at the Bayshore Center at Bivalve, is the most stirring reminder of that boom time. That it's still making cruises up and down Delaware Bay is somewhat of a miracle. During World War II, the Coast Guard commandeered the ship and outfitted it as a fireboat. In 1947, Clyde A. Phillips bought it from the Meerwald family and used it as an oyster dredge. A subsequent owner, Nicky Campbell, would use it as a clam dredge. He worked it 20 years, then the boat ran aground; it remained stuck in the mud for four years.

Meghan Wren saw the boat's potential, bought it for $1, and formed a nonprofit to raise funds to repair it. The Bayshore Center was born. The schooner's restoration cost $900,000; the project took just over two years. The schooner was rechristened and launched on September 12, 1995.

Harbor good for sailor men,
Harbor O.
Tavern good for sailor men,
Tavern O.
Early in the morning,
Tavern O.
Early in the morning,
Give us a drop of brandy.
Tavern good for sailor men,
Tavern O.

Bivalve, near the end of the end of New Jersey, isn't much to look at today—several oyster packing plants, a Rutgers shellfish research laboratory, the Bayshore Center, the Oyster Cracker Café, the Delaware Bay Museum, and the *A. J. Meerwald*.

A presail visit to the Delaware Bay Museum is a must. Displays track Bivalve's emergence as the oyster capital of the world. "It was the railroad that made Bivalve and the surrounding communities boomtowns—much like the Wild West—New Jersey's last economic frontier," according to one display.

A movie about local oystermen can be viewed in the theater. "The smell of the river—that's something that will stay with me forever," one oysterman muses.

A. J. Meerwald passengers are reminded to use the restroom alongside the Bayshore Center beforehand; there are no facilities on the boat. One of the boxcars used to ship out oysters in Bivalve's heyday now serves as the center's restrooms.

Before the tall ship casts off, Steinke recites "The Yarn of the Nancy Bell," a mid-1850s ballad that could be called the cannibal version of Coleridge's "Rime of the Ancient Mariner." In "Nancy Bell," all but one of the crew members end up in the cooking pot.

'Twas on the shores that 'round our coast
From Deal to Ramsgate span
That I found alone on a piece of stone
An elderly naval man.
His hair was weedy, his beard was long,
And weedy and long was he,
And I heard this wight on the shore recite
In a singular minor key,
"Oh, I am a cook, and a captain bold,
And the mate of the Nancy brig,
And a bosun tight, and a midshipmite,
And the crew of the captain's gig."

Steinke recites the yarn in rollicking fashion, not missing a word—no easy feat because the ballad is 23 verses and 92 lines long. When he's done, the crew casts off the lines, and the tall ship heads regally into the bay. The Johnson Girls serenade passengers with chanteys such as "Riley" and "The Johnson Girls," the menhaden net-hauling chantey the group is named after. The group calls itself "the foremost all-woman maritime song group in the world." Folk music legend Pete Seeger once told them, "Where have you girls been? You're first rate!"

Johnson Girls is a mighty fine girls.
Walk around honey, walk around.

The group has been together since 1997; their four CDs include *The Johnson Girls, On the Rocks, Fire Down Below,* and *On Deck & Below.* Shipboard programs on the *A. J. Meerwald* in 2018 also included mariachi and Irish folkloric music and a steel drum band.

We pass East Point Lighthouse, heading upstream.

"We'll get as far as we get," Steinke says. "Probably get as far as Shellpile." There is a welcoming wind, but no sooner does Steinke cut the engine than the wind dies down.

"What happened to our wind?" he says. "It decided to quit." He's been the tall ship's captain since mid-March 2018. "I've been [piloting] tall ships the past 13, 14 years. West Coast, East Coast, Viking ship in the North Sea . . ." He is also the coauthor of a children's book, *The Greatest Captain in the World.*

Not even a breeze stirs the sails. "We're going nowhere," Steinke says. "It's a beautiful spot to be nowhere, though."

Indeed. Just being on the water is treat enough.

The *A. J. Meerwald* at dock.

Friendly winds or not, this is one boat that gets around. NJ ports of call in 2019 included St. Michaels, MD; Baltimore; Lewes, DE; Cape May; Greenwich; Alpine; and Atlantic Highlands. It also sailed from Bristol, PA, and New Castle, DE, and participated in the Great Chesapeake Bay Schooner Race.

The Johnson Girls take a break, then First Mate Josh Scornavacchi talks about the bay's rich history: in the 1930s, there might have been 300-500 schooners on the water at one time. The cruise, alas, ends all too soon. The crew wishes us well. The Johnson Girls—their next gig would be the Folk Music Society of New York's Fall Folk Music Weekend—sell their CDs. Passengers trudge across the gravel parking lot to their cars at this lonely but atmospheric end of New Jersey.

Whiskey good for sailor men,
Whiskey O.
Early in the morning,
Whiskey O.
Early in the morning,
Give us a drop of whiskey.

Bivalve may look remote on the map, but getting there is not difficult (bring a county map; your GPS may not reliable). From Route 47, follow Mauricetown Crossway Road (Route 670) to Route 649, which dead-ends in Port Norris. At the stop sign, turn left for Shellpile or right for Bivalve. Reach the latter by making a left onto Memorial Avenue and follow it about a half-mile to a stop sign, then turn right. All there is to see in Bivalve is just down that road.

HOMEMADE AND GOOD

RODRIGO DUARTE LEADS THE WAY down into a basement, unlocks one padlocked door, then another, and reaches for a switch. The fluorescent lighting casts an eerie reddish glow on this face and the product in the 55-degree room—pigs on multiple-knotted ropes hanging from the ceiling.

"Here we have about $200,000 worth of pata negra," he says matter-of-factly. That's $200,000 worth of what Duarte calls "the highest-quality pork available in the world," the purebred or *puro alentejano* pigs he raises on a farm in Pennsylvania and sells at Caseiro e Bom, his meat-mad store in Newark's Ironbound.

"Pata Negra $499 / lb, 3-year age," reads a chalked message on a board. That's $499.00 a pound, not $4.99. On my first visit to the store, one of Duarte's employees happily sliced off sample after sample of the high-priced ham like it was bologna from the local supermarket.

There is no high-tech equipment in the humidity- and temperature-controlled basement aging room. "I don't go by computers; I go by experience," Duarte says. "I'm trying to replicate it the old-fashioned way." His cell rings; the connection fails. It rings again—apparently a potential buyer from Germany. The word is out about "Don Rodrigo" in the Ironbound.

"What he's doing is artisanal in the perfect sense of the word," says Vince Baglivo, marketing director for the Ironbound Business Improvement District. "He's making products maybe no one else is making."

The Portuguese are the biggest ethnic group in the Ironbound; Ecuadorians are second, according to Baglivo. The Ironbound is New Jersey's best-known food neighborhood, home to some 200 restaurants, markets, cafés, and specialty food stores. Take a train to Newark Penn Station, step outside, on Ferry Street, and you're there.

Duarte is the official breeder of *puro alentejano* pigs in the U.S. for the government of Portugal. It took the native of Portugal ten years to acquire permission to ship ten live *puro alentejano* pigs to the United States. Those 10 pigs—8 females, 2 males—were flown from Lisbon to JFK, then spent 30 days in quarantine in upstate New York.

"I have paperwork; I will show you downstairs," Duarte says. The pigs on his farm are cosseted and fussed over and fed a strict diet.

"Our pigs breed in the field; they drop babies in the field," Duarte explains. "We give them vegetables, no grain. We [fatten] them [up] with acorns and chestnuts in the field." Those are

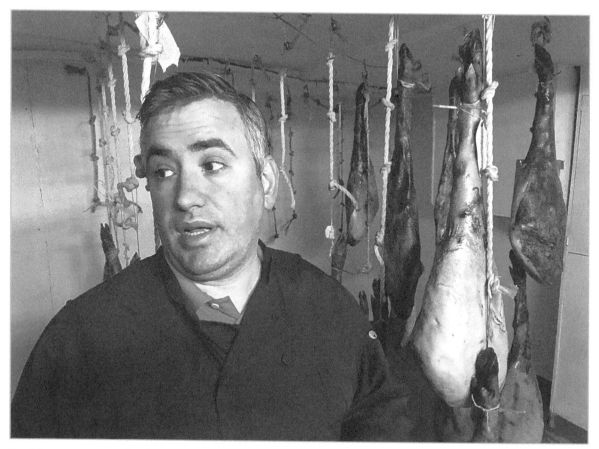

Rodrigo Duarte inside the subterranean pata negra storage room at Caseiro e Bom

imported acorns and nuts from Portugal and Spain, the critical diet required to maintain the highest level of quality, according to Duarte. The nut-based diet is the basis of the sought-after intramuscular fat *puro alentejano* pigs are prized for.

Duarte's original 10 pigs are still alive and kicking. Of his pigs in general, Duarte says, "I don't think I could stab a knife in them. I love them."

Eventually they are sent to a local slaughterhouse; Duarte doesn't want to witness the act firsthand. Duarte says he was "born" into a farm family, one of nine siblings, all brothers. He's from Cantanhede, in central Portugal.

"Tons of fields of potatoes, tons of acres of green peas. Cabbage. Broccoli. In the backyard was where we bred the pigs. We'd slaughter a couple pigs a year to make hams, to make chorizo, to make traditional charcuterie." All the meat was for family use—"there were 13 mouths [to feed]." His mother, who passed away two years ago of lung cancer, would bake 100 pounds of rolls every week.

He was eight years old when he first killed a pig; it was part of a traditional daylong celebration called *matança*. "It's not that I had any desire to kill it," he told Voices of New York. "I just wanted very much to be part of that tradition."

Duarte worked in a butcher shop, studied at a tourism and hospital school in Lisbon, and opened his own butcher shop, but that didn't do well. A friend who worked for Seabra's said he should move to the U.S. and work for the Portuguese-owned supermarket chain. Duarte ran the butcher shop at a Seabra's in Newark, then worked for Kings in Short Hills. In 2006, he opened Caseiro e Bom—Portuguese for "Homemade and Good"—in Newark's Ironbound. He made fact-finding missions to Portugal, meeting with butchers and shop owners, and was determined to bring *puro alentejano* to the United States. He worked with a lab in Portugal to import the semen and breed his pigs here. He shows U.S. Customs records of pigs, even breaks out a semen sample collector.

Pata negra—Portuguese for "black hoof"—is not an official classification; it's a name popularly given to the high-end pigs, which may or may not be *puro alentejano*. Alentejano pigs are 100 percent purebred and are registered in the Portuguese pedigree book for pigs, section Alentejano breed, a guarantee the animals were bred and raised according to government rules.

Inspectors from Portugal come over once a year to inspect and tag Duarte's Alentejano pigs. The shop owner often takes his five-year-old son to the farm to feed the pigs; smartphone photos show he's having a blast doing it. "When he was like three years old, one of the days, I took him to the farm and he saw me walking around the pigs. He goes, 'Daddy what are you doing?' I said, 'I am checking every single pig to see if they're all OK.' A week after, he went with us. He was walking around the pigs. I said, 'What are you doing?' He said, 'Dad, I already checked every one of them; they're good.'"

Celebrity chefs have taken notice of what the soft-spoken Ironbound butcher is doing. He hopes to sign an agreement with Wolfgang Puck. At the Charcuterie Masters competitions in Queens, he was awarded Best Ham in 2016 and 2017. At the Pig Island competition in Brooklyn in 2016, he was awarded Best Traditional Food and Best in Show. In 2017, Best in Show. In 2018, Best Whole Hog.

"What I did was something out of the box," he said of one competition. "Pig bladder. I cooked . . . the pig bladder over an open flame [and] made a nice sandwich." He calls up photos from his phone. "Look how beautiful."

By the end of 2020, he figures to have 1,000 pigs. Which means more acreage, somewhere. "We don't have enough room here. I have to expand. We have to crawl before we walk, walk before we run."

The Ironbound store is a vision of the piggy pearly gates, with hams hanging from the ceiling and packages of chorizo, serrano ham, duroc, and sausage in bins. There's beef, too—*maminha* (sirloin tips), *cupim brasileiro* (beef humps), and *fraldinha* (skirt steak). Cans, boxes, and packages of imported cookies, sweets, and gaily colored tins of El Avion Pimenton Dulce Ahumado—smoked mild paprika. Behind the counter are three types of ham, lengthwise—*puro alentejano*, $499 a pound; American-bred duroc, $50 a pound; and traditional smoked ham, $30 a pound.

"We have to have price points," Duarte explains. "Different flavor profiles. All of them are good." He smiles. "I have 100 hams smoking. I can show you if you want to see." So off we go down the street and to another basement, thick with the sensuous aroma of smoked meat.

"Here we roast pigs [the] old-fashioned [way]. Here we smoke some of our sausage [in an] old-fashioned smokehouse. Right now, we are smoking country ham.

"You don't see a lot of these anymore, right?" he adds, smiling. I just want to pull up a chair and breathe in that pungent woodsmoke.

Duarte hopes to offer "intensive hands-on charcuterie classes." He's held less intricate classes in previous years, with people flying in from Illinois, California, and other states. He talks animatedly of food quality and safety, that we must spend more time examining what we eat and where it comes from.

"Food needs to change. We need to have our children and grandchildren have better food than we do . . . If we don't act, one day we're not going to know what we're eating anymore." He's now studying veterinary medicine "to be more knowledgeable" and to be a veterinary technician.

"Right now I have 30 years on this job. I don't see myself doing anything else besides meat."

THE VIEW FROM HIGH POINT

I AM STANDING AT THE top of New Jersey, the only person up here on this lovely late summer day, the sky a flawless bright blue, the moon a ghostly white dot in the distance. Pennsylvania to one side, New York to the other, New Jersey all around.

Col. Anthony R. Kuser and Susie Dryden Kuser donated the land for High Point State Park, which was dedicated as a park in 1923. The landscaping was designed by the Olmsted Brothers of Boston; the brothers' father was Frederick Law Olmsted, the designer of Central Park. There isn't any gimmickry or high tech up here, just several Tower Optical Co. spotting scopes, a scattering of picnic tables, and that splendid view. At 1,803 feet, High Point is more a hill than a mountain, but at least it's higher than the highest elevations in 10 states, and the only one of all 50 to be called simply High Point.

The breathtaking view from atop High Point State Park

Which comes as no surprise. We don't mess around in New Jersey. We come right to the point. Our honesty—some would say bluntness—is our calling card. Are we rude? Sometimes, and it's probably just because we're having a bad day. It does take a certain sense of humor, a jaunty je ne sais quoi, to get through the day, especially when you spend half of it sitting in traffic. If I ever move out of New Jersey, I will not miss the Garden State Parkway one little bit, or least the stretch through Essex and Union counties. Once I get over the Driscoll, I breathe easier. Most of the time anyway.

But back to High Point. It's the best proof that New Jersey defies the stereotypes that have beset this state for decades. Ugly. Smelly. Crowded. Traffic snarls. Garbage dumps. Dilapidated warehouses. Polluted rivers. This is the view first-timers get when they fly into Newark Liberty International Airport, so of course they think the rest of the state must be like this.

No wonder we are the most mocked, maligned, misunderstood state. People—outsiders—just don't know any better. They haven't the time nor desire to wander much afield. Even New Jerseyans are guilty of this; I bet eight out of ten North Jerseyans have never visited the Great Falls in Paterson, the state's greatest natural wonder. How many of us have spent a full day—or stayed overnight—in the Pine Barrens? Count this writer, who has probably seen more of New Jersey than anyone, guilty too. Until the Pinelands canoe trip for this book, the last extended length of time I spent in the Pine Barrens was a winter camping trip 10 years previous. I drive through the Pinelands all the time, but it's not the same as spending quality time there.

How many of us have driven to High Point? It's hardly an arduous trip—a short turnoff from Route 23. Along the way are wooded vistas, picnic areas and, somewhat improbably, a beach.

The view from High Point this particular day is breathtaking. I'm up above the noise and crowds and traffic jams in the nation's most densely populated state. At some point, I have to get back in my Jeep and make the long drive home. But I'm going to stay a few minutes longer and enjoy the view, the otherworldly peace and quiet, the snap of that crisp, clean New Jersey air. OK, so maybe I'm getting carried away a bit here. This much is true: I love this state, even if it drives me bonkers and batty much of the time. There was a time in my life when I dreamed of moving to Montana. Well, I'm sure glad that dream didn't come true. What would I have written about out there? Big empty, lonely spaces.

There's so much more here. What other state packs more scenic wonder and cultural/ethnic diversity into such a tiny, tidy package? From swamps to Shore, refineries to wildlife refuges, we have it all.

I hope this book shows you the real New Jersey, or at least one free of the usual clichés and stereotypes. I hope it encourages you to explore more of the 8,700 or so square miles out there; "The 40 Best Places to Visit in New Jersey" chapter is a good jumping-off point.

I hope the state comes alive in this book, and that it encourages you to seek out my other books and all the excellent books about New Jersey.

So thanks for reading. I'm going to stay at High Point a bit longer. The view up here—well, I already told you about that view.

I've got the place to myself, and I don't want to drive down the hill just yet.

THE 40 BEST PLACES TO VISIT IN NEW JERSEY

THIS BOOK IN ONE SENSE is a travel book, as it takes you to corners of New Jersey you may not have thought existed. Here's a rundown of my 40 favorite places to visit.

Absecon Lighthouse, Atlantic City. Other lighthouses—Barnegat Light, Twin Lights, Hereford Inlet—get more publicity, but my favorite is Absecon Lighthouse, which is not in Absecon at all but Atlantic City. It's the country's third-tallest lighthouse, and the tallest in New Jersey, at 171 feet. It was first lit on January 15, 1857. Walk 229 steps to the watch room for a breathtaking 360-degree panorama of beach and casino.

Adventure Aquarium, Camden. There's plenty to do on the Camden waterfront—concerts at the BB&T Pavilion, tours of the Battleship New Jersey, and getting up close and personal with sharks, penguins, hippos, stingrays—8,500 marine animals in all. The aquarium boasts the largest collection of sharks on the East Coast, including the only great hammerhead shark in the United States. It's also the only aquarium in the world to exhibit hippos. What are you waiting for? There are also behind-the-scene encounters; in one, you don a wet suit and swim with the sharks. I think I'll pass on that one.

Albert Music Hall, Waretown. Old-timey bluegrass music has long been a favorite of mine, and there may not be a better place in the country to hear it than Albert Music Hall. It's named for two brothers, Joe and George Albert, who invited local musicians to their small, secluded deer cabin to pick and sing on Saturday nights. Several musicians would later rent a big room at Waretown Auction; it burned down in 1992. The new Albert Music Hall, on Wells Mills Road, opened in 1997. Shows are held every Saturday night year-round.

Amish Market at Mullica Hill, Mullica Hill. My favorite food market in New Jersey, this market beckons you with its heady aroma of fresh bread, donuts, soft pretzels, nuts, cheese, meats, and more. Donuts to the right, just inside the front door; breads and pies from Beiler's just ahead of you. My favorite section: the rotisserie chickens at the Chicken Shack (formerly Yoder's), in the back. The last time I was there, I picked one up and didn't eat it until eight hours later. It was still wonderful. There are a handful of Amish markets in New Jersey; this is the best.

Bayway, Linden. New Jersey's most magnificent man-made sight, Bayway (formally Phillips 66 Bayway Refinery) is especially magnificent at night, with the pipes, stacks, and towers lit up in surreal, *Blade Runner*–ish fashion. By day, immense puffy clouds of vapor billow from Tinkertoy-like structures. Built in 1909, Bayway, which processes mainly light, low-sulfur crude oil from Canada and West Africa, is the nation's oldest refinery and the East Coast's largest. It sits on 1,300 acres of land and there are 675 miles of pipe. The New Jersey Turnpike runs right through it, which provides those incredible nighttime views.

Bergenline Avenue, West New York, Union City. One of the state's great food streets, Bergenline Avenue and environs feature a head-spinning array of Central and South American restaurants, markets, bodegas, cafés, and bakeries. Dulce de Leche is a spacious Argentinian bakery in West New York with an amazing chocolate mousse cake. The Argentina Bakery in Union City is tiny but no less wonderful. La Pola makes the nation's best Cuban sandwich, according to Food Network personality Carl Ruiz. For steak sandwiches, try Dos Amigos in West New York. Best advice: just wander down Bergenline and nearby streets (Palisade, Summit, etc.) and let your nose be your guide.

Bivalve. It's a long way from just about anywhere, but Bivalve, apart from having one of New Jersey's most colorful town names, makes for a great day trip. The *A. J. Meerwald*, New Jersey's official tall ship, is here, at the Bayshore Center at Bivalve. The center features exhibits from when Bivalve was an oyster industry boomtown. There isn't much to "see" in Bivalve, but that's just the point. It's an atmospheric slice of New Jersey not destined to appear on any state tourism calendar.

Cape May Zoo, Middle Township. A spectacular wild kingdom near the end of the Garden State Parkway, Cape May Zoo opened 40 years ago and yet remains a relative secret to most New Jerseyans. It's home to 500-plus animals—crocodiles, giraffes, parrots, flamingos, zebras, cranes, bison, elk, a black bear, a lion, and much more. The zoo spends about $200,000 in food a year, including $30,000 worth of produce, $25,000 in meat, and $30,000 in hay. The snow leopards love their raw beef, the reptiles their rats and mice, and the macaws are picky about their palm nuts. Did I mention admission is free? Yes, free.

Clinton. The town is not on this list because I once lived there, but because it's so darn . . . cute. Shops line the picturesque Main Street, and the South Branch Raritan River provides a scenic backdrop. The Red Mill Museum Village, on the other side of the river, might be the most popular New Jersey postcard scene ever. Good subs at Ye Olde Sub Base, by the way. Clinton is a great gateway to the rest of beautiful Hunterdon County.

Commercial fishing ports. New Jersey's commercial fishing industry is a $200-million-a-year business, with ports in Bedford, Barnegat Light, Port Norris, Atlantic City, Point Pleasant Beach, and Cape May. Viking Village, in Barnegat Light, is particularly noteworthy; there are dock tours in the warmer months, and you can buy fish right off the boats. Same goes for the smaller Belford Seafood Co-op (see separate chapter, "At the Dock of the Bay"), where fluke is king. Forget about those "fresh fish" signs at your local supermarket; fish doesn't get any fresher than at one of the ports' markets.

Cooper River Park, Pennsauken. If you've heard of Cooper River Park, it's probably because of the prestigious rowing events held there, plus the Cooper River Yacht Club. But the 346-acre park is an urban oasis, with bike paths, cinder track, softball fields, picnic areas, volleyball courts, pavilions, even a pooch park. You can also rent paddle boats and kayaks. Or just pull up a bench and enjoy the peace and quiet.

Cowtown, Pilesgrove. The nation's longest-running weekly rodeo is in . . . New Jersey? You bet. Cowtown traces its roots to 1929, when Stony Harris started putting on rodeo shows at the county fair. Today, you can watch real live cowboys and cowgirls compete in bull riding, steer wrestling, barrel racing, and other events; you'll swear you're in Montana or Wyoming. It's open every Saturday night from Memorial Day weekend through the last Saturday in September.

Delaware & Raritan Canal State Park. Most of the time, I find myself driving along this scenic, shady oasis through, say, Titusville; next time I'm going to get out of the car and get some exercise. The park, 70 miles long in two sections from Frenchtown to Trenton and from Trenton to New Brunswick, is paradise for walkers, hikers, fishermen, canoeists, and folks who just want to lose themselves for a while. Beside the paths, there are tender houses, wooden bridges, and remnants of locks, a reminder of an age when freight moved by mule teams or steam tugboats. Scenic spots include Washington Crossing, Bull's Island, and Griggstown.

Delsea Drive-In, Vineland. New Jersey is the birthplace of the drive-in—the Automobile Drive-In on the Camden-Pennsauken border opened in 1933; admission was 25 cents per person, one dollar for three or more people. The 1950s and 1960s were boom times for drive-ins; scores could be found throughout the state. But when the Hazlet Drive-In closed in 1991, New Jersey found itself without a drive-in—until the Delsea Drive-In, which had closed in 1987, reopened in 2004. Those in-car speakers you'd prop on your window are no more; you tune in the sound on your car radio. But you can set up your lawn chairs outside, and of course, there's a snack bar.

Deserted Village at Feltville, Berkeley Heights. New Jersey's only official deserted village is located, interestingly enough, just off one of the state's busiest highways (Route 78). It's a collection of 10 buildings, all that's left of a long-forgotten quasi-Utopian mill town started by David Felt in the mid-1800s. Felt wanted to improve the workingman's lot, so he built a mill town with a school, church, general store, barn, and blacksmith shop, as well as spacious homes with yards where workers could grow produce. The village later became a resort, which lasted until the early 1900s. Today, it makes for an unforgettable, if somewhat spooky, visit. Park in the lot at the corner of Cataract Hollow Road and Glenside Avenue, and walk down the winding road through a hushed cathedral of trees to the village, with its stately church and grand old houses.

Finns Point National Cemetery / Fort Mott State Park, Pennsville. Finns Point is the final resting place for an intriguing assortment of military veterans: Union guards, Confederate soldiers, German POWs, and World War II veterans are all buried there. Nearby is the caretaker's house where William Reese, who worked at Finns Point, was allegedly killed by Andrew Cunanan, the prime suspect in the murder of fashion designer Gianni Versace. Fort Mott State Park is a scenic spot, with riverfront picnic areas, Finns Point Lighthouse, and the fort.

Gardens at Wyckoff, Wyckoff. This may the state's least-known romantic spot, an oasis of peace and quiet beauty minutes from the Garden State Parkway. The 13-acre property was deeded to the township by the late Warner "Bud" Brackett. There are about 500 or so roses in a gated garden; make sure to explore the entire grounds. Don't go searching for a website or Facebook page; there isn't any.

Goat Hill Overlook, West Amwell. It takes some getting to—you don't want to drive that brand-new Lamborghini up the rocky road to the parking lot—but Goat Hill Overlook, overlooking the Delaware River and Lambertville, is worth the trek. It was used by both Gen. Washington and Gen. Cornwallis during the Revolutionary War to view opposing troop activity up and down the river. Goat Hill Road is accessible from Pleasant Valley Road, off Route 29, or from Lambertville itself.

The Great Auditorium, Ocean Grove. It's the state's most wondrous wooden structure, soaring and sweeping, often alive with the sound of music. Ocean Grove was founded as a Methodist camp meeting in 1869. The auditorium was built by shipbuilders, which accounts for its boat-like interior. The grand organ boasts 11,000 pipes, and it's something to hear. There are worship services and concerts at the auditorium; a recent, and unlikely, one was the Ultimate Queen

Celebration, a tribute to the guys behind "Bohemian Rhapsody." Nearby is Ocean Grove's summertime "tent city," one of New Jersey's quirkiest, most delightful sights.

Great Falls, Paterson. I'll be forever amazed by the number of New Jerseyans who've never visited the Great Falls. Start with a hot dog at legendary Libby's, then walk across the street and onto the bridge overlooking the falls. Prepare to be blown away. Spectacular, majestic, awesome—supply your own adjective. Don't miss the Great Falls Historic District Cultural Center nearby. I'm on a personal mission to get every last Jerseyan to visit the state's greatest natural wonder.

Haddonfield. Nearby Collingswood is the It destination, but I like Haddonfield more. It's more tranquil, more historic-looking, and what other town has a dinosaur downtown? That's *Hadrosaurus foulkii*, which was the most complete dinosaur skeleton unearthed anywhere in the world when it was discovered in 1858. The Indian King Tavern Museum marks the site where New Jersey became a state and the great seal of the state was adopted. Sweet tooth? Indulgence Cupcakery makes great cupcakes.

High Point State Park. 1,803 feet is not much for your state's highest point, but at least we're higher than Missouri, Ohio, and eight other states. There are 50 miles of trails within the park, and the drive to the top snakes through beautiful woods and fields. There's even a beach, somewhat improbably, on the way up.

Insectropolis, Toms River. If you are absolutely terrified by bugs, you might want to stay away from here. The state's "bugseum" features thousands of beautiful and frightening-looking insects, both live and preserved. Iridescent-blue butterflies, ghostly walking sticks, sinister-looking scorpions. A dozen kinds of tarantulas, including the oddly named giant white-kneed and Mexican red rump. Displays tell the creepy-crawly story of the world under our feet.

The Ironbound, Newark. New Jersey's greatest food neighborhood, with about 200 restaurants, cafés, bakeries, and markets. It's more than just Spanish and Portuguese eateries; Mexican and Central and South American eateries are in abundance. Start on Ferry Street and work your way down. Popular Fish Market lives up to its name. Ferry Street BBQ is the best-known barbecue joint. For Brazilian food, try Delicias De Minas. Café Pão de Queijo makes awesome cheese bread. Suissa Bakery is well under the radar but wonderful. I could go on. Take a train to Newark Penn Station; Ferry Street is steps away.

Lakota Wolf Preserve, Columbia. This jaw-dropping slice of the Wild Kingdom, which opened in 1998, is home to about 20 Arctic, timber, and tundra wolves who roam about in their spacious enclosure, spooky eyes and all, never failing to evoke *ooh*'s and *ahh*'s from visiting school groups. Those wolves are lean eating machines; they go through 50,000 pounds of meat a year. It all started when Dan and Pam Bacon acquired two wolf pups from North Dakota and opened a wolf facility in Colorado; they relocated to New Jersey in 1997, opening Lakota a year later. It's open year-round, and you must make a reservation on weekdays; no appointments are necessary for weekend tours. The preserve is reached by a half-mile trail from the parking lot at Camp Taylor Campground; there is also a shuttle bus.

Lambertville. When I ranked New Jersey's best small towns, Lambertville came out on top, with its scenic riverfront setting, lively arts community, loads of shops, an eclectic mix of restaurants, and a funky sister city (New Hope) that's a state, but a short walk, away. Hunterdon County is packed with scenic small towns, but none offer quite the complete package that Lambertville does. The state's most unique bar, the Boat House, is here. It's a trip; you're not allowed to stand at the bar, and if it reaches capacity you'll have to wait outside until things open up. For great pizza, visit Liberty Hall. Steps away is Owowcow Creamery, winner of nj.com's best-ice-cream showdown. For Middle Eastern food, Marhaba.

Liberty Science Center, Jersey City. For starters, it boasts the largest planetarium in the Western Hemisphere—the Jennifer Chalsty Planetarium, capable of a mind-blowing 300 trillion colors. The center manages to combine the serious with fun: for example, it hosted a petition to get the state to recognize *Streptomyces griseus* (a soil-dwelling bacteria) as the official state microbe. Crawl through the 80-foot-long, pitch-black Touch Tunnel, scale the world's first suspended climbing play space; gaze in wonder at naked mole rats and leaf-cutter ants; climb a rock wall; create combinations of colors, sounds, and scents on the Dream Machine—there seem to be a thousand different things to do here. Great gift shop too. At night, wander across the park for an unforgettable, impossibly romantic view of the glittering Manhattan skyline.

Little India, Iselin. Oak Tree Road in Woodbridge and Edison might be New Jersey's most atmospheric street; just a two-block stretch in Iselin is packed with nearly 100 stores of dizzying and often delicious variety: sweets and snacks shops, jewelry stores, music stores, clothing stores, hair salons, dancing schools, shipping firms, and more. In the late 1980s, Oak Tree Road was a collection of bars and pizzerias, with a barbershop, a hardware store, and some other businesses. In 1987, Chetan Nayar opened Sona Jewelers; a friend opened a restaurant nearby. They were two of the first four Indian-owned businesses here. Patel Brothers is a legendary market, Dimple's Bombay Talk a lively café; go to Chowpatty Chavana & Sweet Mart for one-stop sweets shopping.

Loew's Jersey Theatre, Jersey City. Many of Jersey's grand old movie palaces have fallen into disrepair or have been demolished. Not Loew's Jersey Theatre near Journal Square, a magnificent movie palace that still shows films. It was billed as "The Most Lavish Temple of Entertainment in New Jersey" when it opened its doors in September 1929. The theater fell into disrepair in the 1980s; more than $1 million in repairs have restored it to its former splendor. Check loewsjersey.org for films and events.

Lucy the Elephant, Margate. The nation's only six-story elephant (I don't know of any five- or seven-story ones either) stands regally on her oceanfront perch. Built in 1881 from a million pieces of timber and 12,000 square feet of tin, Lucy was one of three elephants designed by real estate developer and engineer James Vincent de Paul Lafferty. The other two are long gone; Lucy remains. You walk up one of her legs to reach the museum and gift shop upstairs. Oh, about her name: Lucy has tusks, which in real life are found only on male elephants.

Luna Parc, Sandyston. New Jersey's most flamboyant, madcap home is Luna Parc—part fairy-tale castle, part rococo extravagance with its wonderfully eccentric mishmash of turrets and towers. It's the work of artist Ricky Boscarino, who started transforming the once-derelict hunting cabin in 1989, adding doors, windows, towers, turrets, and rooms now filled with wonders and curiosities—knights in armor, two massive doors from a Beijing salvage yard, stuffed animals, 100-year-old back scratchers and enough folk art, artifacts, ephemera, souvenirs, and knickknacks to create one marvelous oddball museum. Luna Parc (named not after the long-gone Coney Island amusement park but after a small amusement park near Rome) is not open to the public except during open house weekends. See lunaparc.com for details.

Main Street, Paterson. Another great food street, Main Street is chockablock with Middle Eastern restaurants, bakeries, and markets. Nablus Sweets and Pastries, Fattal's Syrian Bakery, and Nouri Brothers Market are legendary. The compact-sized Nayef Sweets serves up my favorite pastries, and the mint lemonade at Al Basha is the best lemonade ever created; it's that incredible. One block from Main Street, on Getty Avenue, is Al Raouche, which makes a great lamb kebab sandwich; it was the best thing I ate in all of 2018.

Millville Army Air Field, Millville. The state's least-known former military base/installation, the Millville Army Air Field was heralded as "America's First Defense Airport" when it opened in August 1941. In 1943, it added a gunnery school for fighter pilots; 1,500 pilots would receive advanced training in the Republic P-47 Thunderbolt. Today, it includes a museum with exhibits, including one on Navajo code talkers and women pilots in World War II. The "Wasps," as they were known (for Women Airforce Service Pilots), ferried new planes from factories to military bases and tested newly overhauled planes. Thirty-eight female pilots were killed during World War II service. There are several planes and equipment on the grounds, and next door is Glass-town Brewing, one of my favorite Jersey craft breweries.

Mount Mitchill, Atlantic Highlands. That's Mitchill, not Mitchell. Mount Mitchill in Atlantic Highlands is named after naturalist and botanist Samuel Mitchill. At 266 feet above sea level, it's the highest natural elevation on the Atlantic seaboard, with jaw-dropping views of Sandy Hook Bay, the Atlantic Ocean, and the Manhattan skyline. Also here is Monmouth County's 9/11 Memorial.

National Guard Militia Museum of New Jersey, Sea Girt. The Intelligent Whale—how could you resist? The 28-foot-long, hand-cranked submarine, designed as a secret weapon for the Union during the Civil War (even though it never saw combat duty) is my favorite exhibit at this little-known museum. You'll also find a seagoing Jeep vehicle—the only automobile to have circumnavigated the globe—plus the only Civil War cannon mounted on a carriage on display in New Jersey. There are photographs, documents, and artifacts from the War for Independence to the present day. It's an endlessly fascinating place.

New Jersey Aviation Hall of Fame Museum, Teterboro. A rocket-powered mail plane, the first American hovercraft (Charles Fletcher's Glide-Mobile, in 1959), a Bell AH-1 Cobra helicopter, the rocket engine that propelled the X-15 to hypersonic speed—these are just a few of the air-craft and exhibits at the New Jersey Aviation Hall of Fame Museum. It's another museum that gets lost in the spotlight around bigger, better-known museums. There are exhibits on the *Hin-denburg* (even actual fragments from the zeppelin), Operation Titanic (a 1944 operation that involved dropping 500 dummies over Normandy to divert Germans from the Allies' actual drop zones), women aviators, and much more. Open Cockpit Weekend, in October and November, is a popular event; you can sit in a cockpit and pretend you're a pilot.

Ocean Drive, Ocean City to North Wildwood. The best drive Down the Shore (what, you thought it was the Garden State Parkway?), this local road winds through Strathmere (with that Jersey rarity, a free beach!), Sea Isle City, Avalon, and Stone Harbor before ending in North Wildwood. The most picturesque sections of the road—much of it known as Ocean Drive—vault over marsh and water through a series of toll bridges (which now accept E-ZPass). Forget your GPS; just follow the gull—the bird appears on Ocean Drive signs.

Ocean View Service Plaza, Garden State Parkway, milepost 18.3. What's a rest stop doing on this list? One that's not even a true rest stop like the others on the parkway and turnpike—there's no separate food concession, although you can grab a hot dog. The reason: the tourism information center, which is one of the best I've seen anywhere in the country. There are brochures, booklets, and guides from every part of the Garden State. And it's the only place on either major highway where you can pick up a free state map. I love maps, and the state maps come in handy when I'm writing stories.

Port Newark / Port Elizabeth. Sure, you can see the container ships and giant mantis-like cranes from the turnpike. But there's nothing like a leisurely drive down Calcutta, Export, Egypt, Dakar, Suez, and the rest of the streets that wind through the port complex. The state's strongest cup of coffee might be at the Sea Port Coffee Shop. There is a scattering of food trucks; try Juanito on Marsh Street (excellent chicken or pork stew) or the Yankee lunch truck at Doremus and Port for a good cheesesteak and even better Greek salad.

Pulaski Skyway, Jersey City to Newark. OK, so maybe you can't really "visit" a bridge or highway, but the Pulaski Skyway is my favorite stretch of road in New Jersey, so it must be on this list. Jet-black and sinuously graceful, it snakes 3.7 miles from Jersey City to Newark. If any highway was made with the warning "Buckle Your Seat Belt" in mind, it's the skyway. Road shoulders are practically nonexistent; changing a tire is a death-defying experience. The view from the top is a landscape worthy of Hieronymus Bosch: derelict warehouses, abandoned cars and boats, belching smokestacks, monumental power plants, sprawling truck terminals and container ship depots, train tracks and drawbridges, mountains of metals and recyclables, barbed wire-topped fences and dead-end roads, all scattered across a terrain—marsh, muck, and swamp—even Mother Nature would disown. There's no other bridge or highway quite like it in the country.

The Raptor Trust, Millington. There is something about seeing a hawk or falcon, or even a plug-ugly vulture, up close and personal. The Raptor Trust, one of the nation's preeminent wild bird rehabilitation centers, features outdoor enclosures with 50–55 permanently crippled birds. Much of the activity here is done behind the scenes; the center takes in and treats a staggering 6,000 or so birds a year. The center is located on 14 acres at the edge of the Great Swamp National Wildlife Refuge. It's open to the public seven days a week.

Silverball Museum Arcade, Asbury Park. Best place to spend a rainy day Down the Shore? This boardwalk arcade, filled with scores of vintage pinball machines and games you can play, all ringing and pinging away. The machines include Discs of Tron (1983, Bally Midway), World Fair (1964, Gottlieb), Space Glider (1959, Williams), Pong (1972, Atari), and Capt. Fantastic (1976, Bally). You can buy daily passes or a $50 VIP membership, which allows you unlimited play for a month plus one guest per visit.

St. Vladimir Memorial Church, Jackson. Next to the Cathedral Basilica of the Sacred Heart in Newark, this may be New Jersey's most magnificent church. The onion-bulb domes glow in the late afternoon sun. In the 1930s, Russian immigrants started gathering at Rova Farms here—first on summer vacations, then in homes they built. Services are held in the majestic church, part of the Russian Orthodox Church Outside of Russia.

State Line Lookout, Alpine. For pure dizzying drama, State Line Lookout in Palisades Interstate Park is hard to beat. Signs warn, "Do not go beyond barricade," because it's a sheer drop of 500-plus feet. Birders love this spot; you'll always see a few with giant zoom-lensed cameras. Just south, at park headquarters, begins Henry Hudson Drive, a memorable, meandering, and vertiginous roller coaster ride. Those afraid of heights, or who shudder at the thought of mere stone walls keeping you from plunging hundreds of feet into the river, would do well to stay away. You also need to watch out for bicyclists, hikers, and falling rock. There's a snack bar at the lookout.

Strawberry Avenue, Commercial Township. This may be my favorite off-the-beaten-track spot in the entire state. Drive to the end of Strawberry Avenue in Commercial Township and take a long, lonely walk on the boardwalk. It takes you past a stark, surreal landscape with stunted trees, a fitful creek, a limitless sea of grass, and the Delaware Bay in the shimmering distance. It looks like the end of the earth. It's a scene guaranteed not to be on any welcome-to–New Jersey postcard.

Sunset Beach, Lower Township. First off, let's pay some respect to Lower, which never seems to get any. Cold Spring Village, the Lobster House, Cape May Airport, the Naval Air Station Wildwood, and the Cape May Lighthouse are all located here. So is Sunset Beach, where the evening flag-lowering ceremony is a Shore tradition and where you can see the concrete ship SS *Atlantus*. One of 12 concrete ships built during World War I, the *Atlantus* ran aground 150 feet off Sunset Beach in 1926 and remains an eerie, remarkable landmark.

Tuckerton Seaport, Tuckerton. One of the state's underpublicized attractions, Tuckerton Seaport is a 40-acre maritime village with 17 historic and re-created buildings connected by a boardwalk and wetlands nature trail. Watch boat builders, decoy carvers, commercial fisher-men, basket makers, and other baymen and women explain their crafts. The seaport also hosts special events year-round: carving classes, beer and food truck festivals, the annual Baymen's Seafood and Music Festival, and the Ocean County Decoy & Gunning Show.

Unshredded Nostalgia, Barnegat. There is nothing quite like this shop on Route 9 in Barnegat. It's a treasure chest of toys, collectibles, posters, photos, toys, magazines, antiques, ephemera, and more. The New Jersey Room is jammed with vintage Jerseyana, and the upstairs room is stuffed with thousands of movie posters and photos. Vintage board games, vinyl records, type-writers, cameras, presidential autographs, sports memorabilia, monster magazines, postcards, dolls—the amount of stuff in here is staggering.

Walpack Center, Walpack Township. It's the town that time forgot, a ghostly reminder of the ill-fated Tocks Island Dam project in the 1960s, when about 8,000 people were evicted from their homes for a dam that eventually was never built. Today, no one lives in the buildings on its Main Street, which include a school, a church, a post office, and several homes. The National Park Service owns all the buildings on Main Street except the school, which serves as town hall for Walpack Township (population: 9). Nestled in a spellbindingly beautiful valley along the Delaware River, Walpack Center is the prettiest town no one lives in that you'll ever visit.

Wildwood boardwalk. Wildwood is the best boardwalk in New Jersey, which makes it the best boardwalk on earth. And it's not just because I spent childhood summers there. It takes the low-rent charm of Seaside, the wholesome family atmosphere of Ocean City, the lore and legend of Atlantic City, and the nostalgic pull of Asbury Park and mashes them all together into one unrivaled package. The Shore's tallest Ferris wheel is here; a ride at night, above the boardwalk's neon-lit magnificence, is an essential Jersey Shore experience.

ACKNOWLEDGMENTS

I MET SO MANY WARM, wonderful people during the course of this book. I want to thank them for letting me into their lives and sharing their knowledge, insight, and wisdom.

Thanks to Torie Fisher at Backward Flag Brewing; Bill Sheehan and the Hackensack River-keeper program; Ted Garry, owner of Boardwalk Rolling Chairs; Marc Oshima at AeroFarms; Dave Tauro and the fishermen at Belford Seafood Co-op; Marcus Crawford and Jonathan Gibbs of the Bro-Ritos food truck; all the demolition derby drivers at New Egypt Speedway; Dan McDonough of the Boost! Co. and Matt Garwood, owner of UMMM Ice Cream Parlor; Brooke Hansson for the street art tour of Jersey City; the crew of the *A. J. Meerwald*; Sam Kolokithas at the Truck Stop Diner; Jessica Fricano at Storybook Land; Rodrigo Duarte at Caseiro e Bom; Ted Volpa at Pinelands Adventures.

Also Dan Mandell and the residents of Monmouth Mobile Home Park; Arvind and Alka Agrawal at EBC Radio; Ruth Rodriguez and the supervisors at the Traffic Management Center; Jaclyn Cherubini, along with the staff and volunteers at the Hoboken Shelter; Shawn Wark and Ed Van Hee at South Jersey Classics; Rob Lucas at Donkey's Place; Stephanie Haines at Pine Island Cranberry Co.; Nancy and John DiCosmo of DiCosmo's Italian Ice; chef Carl Ruiz for the tour of West New York and Union City; and Chris Soucy of the Raptor Trust.

I hope I have done all your lives and stories justice.

INDEX

ABOUT THE AUTHOR

Peter Genovese is a features/food writer for the *Star-Ledger* and nj.com. He is the author of 10 books, including *Roadside New Jersey*, *Jersey Diners*, *The Great American Road Trip: Route 1 Maine to Florida*, *The Jersey Shore Uncovered: A Revealing Season on the Beach*, and *Pizza City*, all for Rutgers University Press; *Roadside Florida*, for Stackpole Books; *Food Lovers' Guide to New Jersey* and *New Jersey Curiosities*, for Globe Pequot Press; and *Jersey Eats* and *A Slice of Jersey*, for Pediment Publishing. Winner of various state press association awards, he was nominated for a Pulitzer Prize for his series on Rwanda. A native of Trenton, he lives Down the Shore.